*May all your memories make you laugh and fill your heart with joy.*

*God Bless*

*Cotton Ketchie*

# Memories

## of a

# Country Boy

## "Cotton" Ketchie

ISBN  0-7414-3588-8

*Published by:*

PUBLISHING.COM

*1094 New DeHaven Street, Suite 100*
*West Conshohocken, PA 19428-2713*
*Info@buybooksontheweb.com*
*www.buybooksontheweb.com*
*Toll-free  (877) BUY BOOK*
*Local Phone (610) 941-9999*
*Fax  (610) 941-9959*

*Printed in the United States of America*

*Printed on Recycled Paper*

*Published  October 2006*

# Dedication

For Vickie,

This book would never have been completed without your help. God bless you for your insight, patience, and perseverance.

# Acknowledgments

First of all, I want to thank God for all the rich blessings He has heaped upon my life. All of them were undeserved. My children and grandchildren have inspired me to preserve these memories. I am eternally grateful to have been blessed with such a great family.

I would like to thank my parents, who are both deceased, for nurturing us children and providing a wonderful home, filled with the fondest of memories. I am eternally grateful to my mother for keeping all the wonderful photographs from our childhood.

I want to especially thank my big brother. Roger, you have always been my hero. You made such a positive impression on me when I was young and were the inspiration for many chapters in this book.

Thanks Laura, for being my big sister and providing many fond memories. Without you, my life would not have been the same. Everybody should be as lucky as I, to have been blessed with such a good brother and sister.

I am thankful that I grew up close to my first cousin, Joe Ketchie. Thanks, Joe for the many daring adventures we shared along the way.

I am extremely grateful that Grandma Ketchie, Uncle Gordon, and Aunt Lib lived near me; and were positive forces in my life that helped me to become what I am today.

Thanks to all of my friends, cousins, aunts, uncles and schoolmates who are mentioned in this book and played an important part in my life.

A special thanks to my friends, Donita, Jo-Ann, Jackie, and Susan who work with me at "Cotton" Ketchie's Landmark Galleries and have taken up the slack while I spent my time writing. Thanks for cheering me on with this project and offering your continued support.

Thanks to O. C. Stonesstreet III for his photographs of the old Belk's Department Store and Main Street, 1957.

Thanks also to Speedy Major and Cheryl Brown Beard for the pictures of Brown's Skating Rink and Pool. Speedy's grandparents were the owners of the legendary Mooresville hangout. His mom, Martha Brown Major, often helped us kids with our skates.

I would like to give a special thanks to Frank Glinski who patiently edited my ramblings and faithfully attempted to correct my English. In some instances, I requested that my Southern vernacular remain intact. Any incorrect usage of grammar featured in this book is totally the author's handiwork.

I especially want to thank my wife, Vickie. The writing of these memoirs would have been impossible had it not been for your encouragement, understanding, immeasurable love, and critical ear. You have been a tremendous help as you critiqued each day's work. You helped smooth out many rough places in my text that I would have probably just left for posterity. You also let me use your computer of which you are very possessive. Thank you also for letting me be me!

# Table of Contents

# Introduction

One day, I wrote about the joys of a simple Christmas experienced by a country boy around the age of nine. I am that country boy. Many people read my simple account of that memorable day and were reminded of their childhood Christmases.

I was encouraged by all, who read that little glimpse of Christmas over fifty years ago, to write more about the humorous days of my youth. What follows is a collection of various events in my life that I found amusing and didn't want to forget. Perhaps there will be some of these stories that will evoke fond memories for the reader. If that happens, then this effort will have been a success.

Cotton Ketchie

# A Country Boy

*Memories of a Country Boy* is a collection of things I remember that affected my life. These are random thoughts that invaded my mind and are in no particular order, but I found them entertaining. The ramblings featured here are my vain attempt to shed some light on what it was like to be raised on a small farm in rural North Carolina in the 1950's.

Time flies when you're having fun. That's what I've always heard, and doggoned if it isn't true. I'm now over sixty years old, but I still remember the good times we had when I was a small boy growing up a couple of miles north of Mooresville, North Carolina. We lived so far back in the country—we had to go toward town to hunt. That's exactly the way we felt, and we often had to do just that. Those two miles in the 1950's seemed far greater then, than they do now. Today, a housing development and the city limits of Mooresville jut right up to where Grandma Ketchie's old, weathered barn finished out its last days.

We weren't exactly poor, but we were definitely financially challenged. The upside was that we grew just about everything we ate so we didn't go hungry. We ate dinner at 12:00 noon and supper at 5:30. That's the way God set things up to be. We never varied much from that schedule—we didn't want to appear to be sacrilegious. With no exceptions, grace was said before every meal. No matter how simple the fare would be, it would be blessed.

Grandma Ketchie's house was just a couple hundred yards behind our home and I would eat with them as often as I could. Aunt Lib was a fantastic cook and I never passed up an opportunity to sample the results of her culinary talent.

Uncle Gordon always said the blessing at Grandma's house. He would start out fairly loud, but the longer he went into it, the lower the volume of his voice would be, and I could never hear him by the time he said, "Amen." After a while, I would look up, and everybody else would already be eating. I would be last again.

I grew up living in a small house beside US Highway 21. That highway was the main thoroughfare between Ohio and Florida in the 1950's. Today, it is NC Highway 115 or Statesville Highway, because that's where it will take you, if you drive north—Statesville. Our house stood about halfway between Bill Overcash's Grocery Store and Carl Harkey's Oak Grove Service Station. Carl never gave much service, but he did pump a lot of gas. He had a few groceries, too; but the store was mainly where men gathered to play Checkers while sitting around the stove.

The Blackwelder Family lived on one side of us, and we shared a driveway with them that circled a huge, oak tree that we Ketchie kids rode round and round on our bicycles. Mrs. Blackwelder grew the most beautiful irises that you ever saw, along the edge of their yard. Mr. Blackwelder taught me how to play a mean game of Checkers.

The Malcolm's house was on the other side of us, and they washed their clothes over a fire in a big, black pot in their backyard. They would do this every Monday—you could count on that. Both Mr. and Mrs. Malcolm dipped snuff everyday, too and that was something else you could count on.

# Mama's Family

Let me start at the beginning and introduce my family. My mother was born Helen Louise Rogers on September 6, 1920. By the way, she didn't like the name Louise at all; so we didn't bring it up very much. Sometimes we would call my mama "Mother", and sometimes we would call my mother "Mama". I never knew why we did that—we just did.

My mother's father was Claude Oren Rogers and her mother was born Lillie Blanche Mills. We called him Papaw and her Mamaw. My mother had four brothers and five sisters. Her brothers were named Gene, Ralph, Horace, and Jack. Her sisters were named Emma, Marie, Margaret, Mary, and Martha. It was a big family.

**Left to right: Ralph, Martha, Horace, Mama, Mary, Mamaw, Jack, Papaw, Emma, Margaret, Gene, and Marie**

Papaw Rogers' farm consisted of ninety-eight acres of woods and rolling fields. Papaw and Mamaw Rogers had a great big house with a long driveway that came out on Statesville Highway, just about where Moor Lanes is today. We couldn't visit them when it rained because the ruts in the red, muddy road, going to their house, would make it impassable. In later years, Highway 150 By-Pass went right by their old home-place. Uncle Gene had a small farm that joined theirs; and today, a housing development called Allison Park, a shopping center, and a McDonald's take in all of their combined properties. The Rogers' place was between Grandma Ketchie's farm and the city limits of Mooresville. I wouldn't say that Mooresville was a real city, but everybody said "city limits" anyway.

A couple of years ago, I found out from Aunt Margaret's husband, Uncle Tom Brantley, that Papaw Rogers was known for taking a drink now and then. Mamaw wouldn't put up with that stuff very much. She was a real religious person and a charter member of Broad Street Methodist Church. She always talked about the evils of tobacco and strong drink, but every time you saw her, she was dipping her Tube Rose Snuff.

Papaw Rogers died in 1946 and Mamaw lived by herself most of the time after that. She died many years later, in 1966. When I first married in October, 1963, my wife, Jean and I lived in a mobile home, under a big walnut tree that was beside her house. The walnuts from that tree made a terrific bang as they fell onto the roof of our mobile home. Living close to Mamaw gave me the opportunity to help her out now and then. I remember thawing the water pipes in her basement one extremely cold winter morning and mowing her huge yard with a small push mower in the summer.

Mamaw Rogers' house featured a long, impressive staircase with a terrific, wide banister we always slid down when we went to visit her. It was almost like it was a law—it was just something that we felt obligated to do. I remember the old Victrola that sat in her front room on a parlor table. I don't think she had but a couple of records, but we would

4

crank that thing up and play *Too Old to Cut the Mustard* and laugh and laugh. We thought that was really something. I heard that old song the other day when some friends and I were playing Bluegrass music. I thought it had long been forgotten.

**Mamaw Rogers' house**

Visiting Mamaw on Sundays was sometimes quite a challenge because she was so hard of hearing. She would have her rocking chair pulled up next to her antique Philco radio and would be listening to some Pentecostal preaching, with the volume turned up so loud that we could hear it when we got out of our car. We would bang on the door and the windows to try to get her to hear us. We often just gave up and went home. When we did get to see her, she chastised us for not visiting.

That was Mamaw!

# Daddy's Family

Daddy's father was Joseph Herron Ketchie and his mother's name was Harriet Ella Brawley. They married on December 26, 1905 and settled on a small farm north of Mooresville.

Around 1912, the Ketchie family was having a difficult time during a severe drought that was taking place in North Carolina. Grandpa heard from one of Grandma's cousins about work that was available on a wheat farm near Pearl, Kansas. Grandpa and Grandma Ketchie loaded up their two children, Gordon and Sarah, and headed west. During this temporary relocation, my daddy was born on March 3, 1913. The man who gave Grandpa Ketchie a job was named Millard Taylor. He and my grandpa became such good friends, that my father was christened Millard Vincent Ketchie, in honor of Mr. Taylor and in gratitude for his friendship.

The severe drought gradually improved in North Carolina, and the Ketchie family moved back home while Daddy was still an infant. The rest of the Ketchies were born in Iredell County, North Carolina. As far as I know, Daddy is the only one who was not born here. He probably would have born here, too—if he'd had anything to say about it.

I went out West in 1993 in search of Pearl, Kansas. The town no longer exists, but I found a grain elevator with *Pearl* written across the top of it—that's all that remains of the town. I asked a local farmer, I met at the grain elevator, if there were any Taylor's that lived nearby. He instructed me to follow him as he led me down a few dusty roads. He finally turned down a long tree-covered driveway that led to an old rock barn where I saw a white-haired man sweeping the yard with a broom. The old fellow looked up from his sweeping as we approached.

I got out of my van and introduced myself to him as Millard Ketchie, from North Carolina. The old fellow quit sweeping, and asked, "Did you ever hear of a Joe Ketchie?" I knew then, we had found the place of my daddy's birth. I related to him that Joe Ketchie was my grandfather.

The gentleman introduced himself as Millard York Taylor. His father was the one who had given my grandpa a job over eighty years ago, and was the man for whom my daddy was named.

**Pearl, Kansas grain elevators**

Mr. Taylor's wife came out of their house and joined in our conversation. She talked with us awhile, went back inside their house, and returned with a photograph album that had pictures of my grandfather and Millard Taylor working together. I had a nice visit with the Taylor's and stayed in touch for years, until York passed away. I think I am the only Ketchie to have ever visited the place of Daddy's birth.

My daddy's family was not quite as big as my mother's family. He only had one brother and three sisters. His brother, Gordon, was five years older than he was. Sarah was next in line, then Daddy, Ruth, and the youngest was Catherine. Aunt Catherine and I had something in common. We each were the baby of our families. The main difference being—I was said to have been spoiled.

**Ruth, Grandma, Sarah, Gordon, Daddy, and Catherine**

When you consider that I am related to the Rogers, the Mills, the Ketchies, and the Brawleys, you're talking about a lot of people. You need to be really careful who you're talking about around me—they're probably my kinfolks.

Daddy's family lived on a small farm that consisted of only fifty-five acres. The Ketchie's place was about a mile and a half north of Papaw Rogers' farm. One pasture had undulating hills that led down to a small branch. There was a big patch of pinewoods that you could walk through and never make a sound because of the soft carpet of pine needles. A huge rock with a little waterfall was in the midst of those woods, and that is where I often sat for hours drawing pictures or doing my homework. It was a beautiful, quiet place that I often think about today.

On the other side of the pinewoods was another pasture where we played our baseball games on Sundays. We were not allowed to play ball on Sunday where we could be seen from the highway. We were told that such a thing would bring shame on our family. (Lord knows, we didn't need that.) The bases were made out of dried cow-pies. Hopefully, they were dried enough, or we had to be really careful when we slid into home plate. There were a few fields for corn, cotton, and the grain crops, too. In my youth, their farm was as near to Heaven as I could imagine.

Grandpa Ketchie died in 1939. I never got to know him because that was before I was born. Uncle Gordon; his wife Aunt Lib; their son, Joe Reid, and Aunt Ruth lived with Grandma and helped run the farm after Grandpa died. Grandma Ketchie's house was like a second home to me and I went there just about every day.

Grandma Ketchie's house was not quite as refined as Mamaw Rogers' big home, but it was a whole lot more comfortable and inviting. We didn't have to be as careful when we visited Grandma Ketchie's house; there weren't as many fancy things to break. The narrow stairs that led to where Aunt Ruth and Joe slept didn't have the big, wide banisters like Mamaw Rogers' stairs did. In fact, their stairs didn't have any banisters at all.

Grandma's room was just to the right of the door that led off from the corner porch. As you entered into the sitting room, Uncle Gordon and Aunt Lib had a room that was on the left. Everyone either gathered in the kitchen or the sitting room where the big stove was located.

A large dining room overlooked the back yard and the granary. I would often go into the dining room and lift the big cloth that covered the food on the table to see what goodies I could find.

**Grandma Ketchie's house**

They just left the food out on the table and covered it after each meal. The dining room was next to the warm, cozy kitchen. There were some cupboards that ran along the entire wall behind the old wood-stove where Aunt Lib cooked her fabulous meals. So much wood had to be carried in everyday that I was probably twelve years old before I found out my name wasn't "Get Wood". There was also a front room that was not used very much until Aunt Ruth won a television set at the grand opening of the Medical Arts Pharmacy in

Mooresville. When the TV was put in the front room; we kids kind of took it over.

They had a barn where the milking was done every morning and evening. It featured a loft where we would make hideouts among the musty bales of hay, and there was a small feed room that held feed and cottonseed in big bins. I remember that cobwebs covered the room, but we never bothered to clean them out. The feed and seed were mixed together and used to feed the cows while they were being milked. A few stables for the cows and horses were on both sides of a large aisle that led to the rear of the barn where there were some more stables. The manure had to be shoveled out of the stables from time to time, and I didn't like that job at all. I usually watched as Roger and Joe carried out this inauspicious task, but I was always there to offer my encouragement. There was also a chicken house, woodshed, smokehouse, corncrib, and granary. Grandma even had a rabbit hutch but I don't ever remember seeing any rabbits in it. I recall there was a brooder shed where the little biddies were kept warm by a big light that Uncle Gordon had rigged up for them. I used to go in there and pick up the little chicks and play with them. To me, this farm was a storybook setting that could not have been more perfect.

Uncle Gordon kept two horses named Nell and Kate. They were used for plowing and pulling the wagon. Nell had a beautiful red roan coat and Kate was jet-black.

My first cousin, Harriet Belk, always liked horses and would ride one of them just about every time she came to Grandma's house. One day Harriet was riding Kate, and that old horse turned her head around and bit Harriet on her leg. Well, Harriet promptly retaliated! She leaned forward and bit Kate on the back of her neck. I don't think that horse ever bit anyone else.

Harriet liked horses so much that she made herself some "trotters" out of old Pet Evaporated Milk cans. She would grab those things in her hands, get down on all fours, and gallop up and down Grandma's driveway. Sometimes you could hear her coming with the "trotters" digging in the dust. It really sounded a lot like a real horse galloping. To make it really authentic, once in a while, she would throw her head back and let loose with a loud whinny.

Uncle Gordon also had an old Mule named Bill. He was a stubborn mule that had never been ridden. Everyone was afraid to even try. As Bill got older, we used him for plowing our garden. I often tried to plow with him, but I couldn't stay between the rows and would start plowing up the plants. Daddy would finally take over the reins and put me back to hoeing.

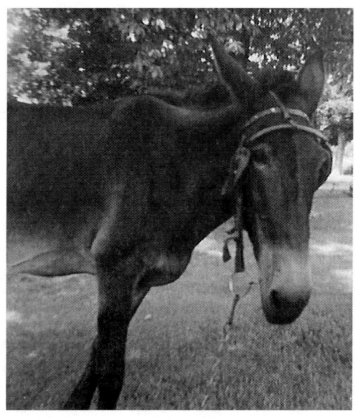

**Our old mule, Bill**

Old Bill was finally retired and spent his last days just hanging around the barn lot—doing what old mules do.

I remember driving the horses and wagon to the cotton field for the last picking of the season. I had the team going pretty fast, and the cotton burrs were flying everywhere. That was a fantastic feeling for a little kid. It was also great to have the cotton crop picked. I never did like picking that stuff. I always said that my back hurt when I picked cotton or anything else that grew low to the ground. I had often heard the saying, "You're in high cotton now", and didn't really know what that meant until I had to pick the doggoned stuff. The cotton plants that were taller were definitely much easier to pick and a whole lot better on my poor back. Being in high cotton was certainly the best place to be. Daddy always said, "You're not old enough for your back to hurt." I didn't know if he had learned that in Kansas or where he had gotten that idea. It didn't take too many years of that cotton-picking stuff for me to know that I would be heading for a career change as soon as possible.

The only thing I remember about cotton picking, that I liked, was when we took the entire crop to Mr. Frank Brawley's cotton gin in Mooresville. I enjoyed riding on top of the cotton as the horse-drawn wagon plodded down Statesville Highway; and knowing all the people in their cars were cussing us for going so slow.

A few years later, Uncle Gordon bought an old, used Ferguson tractor from Mr. A. Y. Neel to replace the horses. We thought we had died and gone to Heaven. We didn't have to feed and water the horses or clean out their stables anymore.

I soon discovered that driving a tractor was a whole lot of fun, but it sure was not the same as having a couple of beautiful horses around, and I missed them sorely. Those noble steeds provided some of my best childhood memories.

# My Family

Daddy and his first cousin, Tom Brantley, grew up together and dated sisters. I think Daddy even dated Mama's sister, Margaret, a time or two. Tom ended up marrying Margaret and Daddy eventually married Mama on January 26, 1936. They decided to elope, so Tom and Margaret went with them to York, South Carolina to be their witnesses. I don't think Mamaw and Papaw Rogers were too keen on the idea of their fifteen year old, little girl marrying a twenty-two year old man.

Until they could find other accommodations, the newlyweds rented a room from Daddy's cousins, Russell and Edna Sherrill, on Brantley Road. Daddy worked in the cotton mill and made only eight dollars a week. He caught a ride to work every morning with Lennie Rappe in his old, Model-A Ford. Daddy told us it snowed nine times that year between their wedding day and spring. I will never forget them telling us about it, either—it never snows like that anymore.

In the fall of 1936, Grandpa Ketchie gave Daddy some lumber to build a little, four-room house on Statesville Highway. This was the house where my parents raised us children and lived out the remainder of their lives.

Nearly four years after they were married, my brother was the first of the Ketchie kids to arrive. He was born on November 15, 1939 and was named Roger Wayne Ketchie. He is five years older than I am, and I guess he always will be. I don't seem to be gaining on him too much. I always thought that he knew everything because he was so much older than I was. I could always trust him then, and I still can today. He was a terrific, older brother and let me tag along with him and his friends on many hair-raising adventures.

My sister came along on July 14, 1941 and was named Laura Jean Ketchie. Laura and I had a lot of fun together and got into about as much trouble as Roger and I did. We always had to do the dishes together and, invariably, would argue about who was washing and who was drying. It was usually arguing over trivial stuff like that, that got us into trouble. I really believe that our parents kept us in the kitchen as long as possible just so they could keep an eye on us. It was great growing up with a brother and sister. All of us Ketchie kids were real close and would take up for one another in a heartbeat.

**Daddy and Mama in the early 1940's**

I remember Mama telling me that she rode on a train all the way to Camp Crowder, Missouri to see Daddy while he was stationed there in the Army. She was pregnant with me at the time and had to stand up just about all the way to Missouri because the train was overcrowded. A kind-hearted soldier gave her his seat about half way there; but later, she lost her seat when she went to the bathroom. The person, who took her seat while she was gone to the bathroom, was not so kind.

I don't know who cared for Roger and Laura while she was gone. I do know that it was a difficult trip for Mama; but people made a lot of sacrifices during the war. (World War II, that is) I don't want anyone thinking that I was born during the Civil War or World War I. I'm not that old!

I was the last of the Ketchie clan to be born and arrived on July 21, 1944, but I don't remember too much about that. (I was awfully young and didn't pay much attention.) Mama and Daddy were really attractive people; so I don't know what happened to the gene pool by the time I came along.

Daddy was in the Army, serving in the Philippine Islands, when I was born. I have always taken consolation in believing that I was the result of one of Daddy's happy furloughs, spent with Mama, before he was shipped overseas. Daddy was concerned that he would not survive World War II and asked Mother to name me "Millard Vincent Ketchie, Jr.", and I have been stuck with that moniker all my life. I've always wondered why Roger wasn't the lucky one to have received that honor—after all; he was the first male offspring. Whatever happened to that tradition? How many little boys did you ever know named Millard? Name just one! I just might as well have been named Sue. I got into a lot of fights over that name.

I think it was around 1939 when a neighbor, Charlie Sherrill, started calling my daddy "Bob". I wish somebody would have called me something sensible like that. My hair was extremely white, and I wanted to have dark hair so desperately that I could hardly stand it. I never knew anyone with hair the color of mine, and it was always a sore spot with me. Mr. Blackwelder sometimes called me "Whitey", and I didn't like that, at all. Then, he called me "Cotton Top" to really upset me. By the time I was in the tenth grade, a lot of people were calling me "Cotton" because my hair was so white. I didn't like that, either; but some of the girls thought it was kind of cute; so I just let the name, "Cotton", stick.

The first photograph was made of me when I was around four weeks old. Mama was holding me on her lap and Roger and Laura were standing on each side of her. It looked like a nice day because the picture was made outside and everyone was smiling except me—I hadn't learned how yet. I was a handsome devil and a lazy one, too. Look at me; just lying in her lap like I didn't have anything to do.

**Laura, Mama, Roger, and me**

Mama had a very difficult time while Daddy was in the Army. She had three small children to clothe and feed on the twenty-one dollars a month that Daddy sent home. Gas, sugar, and a lot of other commodities were rationed. Times were extremely hard on just about everyone.

**Posing with Daddy in his uniform in 1945**

Daddy was discharged from the Army in 1945. He was in his thirties when he enlisted and was one of the oldest men in his outfit. He made the rank of Technical Sergeant and received the Purple Heart while serving our country.

**Happy me, at three**

I don't remember very much about my life when I was really young. I must have been a happy boy by the looks of my early pictures. I believe I was about three years old when this picture was taken of me on my tricycle.

Our car shed is visible behind me and, as you can see, the ground is bare where we kids kept the grass worn down to nothing. Our back yard was a great place to play in the dirt and ride my tricycle to my little heart was content.

The following photograph was made while we were visiting Uncle Tom and Aunt Margaret Brantley at their new house, on what is now Highway 21 By-pass, about 1947.

This is the only photograph I can find that features all five of us together. I am the little white-headed boy displaying the look of authority with my hand on my hip.

**Daddy, Mama, Roger, Laura, and me**

My fifth birthday was very special to me. I can still recall running down the dusty driveway to Grandma's house on my bare feet. Aunt Ruth was sitting on the corner porch with a wrapped present in her lap. I was hoping beyond hope that it might be for me. After all, it was my birthday. She gave me a hug, wished me happy birthday, and then handed me the pretty package. I couldn't believe my eyes when I opened the gift. It was the most beautiful wallet I had ever seen in all of my five years. It had a picture of a cowboy wearing a red shirt sitting astride a bucking bronco. The sky behind the cowboy was bright royal blue and he was wearing a big white hat. (All good cowboys wore white hats.) Aunt Ruth pointed out the zipper that went all the way around the wallet. She said it was put there to prevent all my money from falling out. Heck, I never had any money to worry about falling out. Well, I unzipped the wallet and looked inside and found a brand new one dollar bill with George Washington on the front of it staring back at me. I almost cried. That was the first folding money I ever had in my life. I was one proud little boy. I will always remember Aunt Ruth for that act of kindness.

When we were really young, there were only two bedrooms in our little house. I had to sleep in a small bed with Roger while Laura slept in an even smaller one in the corner of our room. I recall that our mattress was made of straw. It made noises when we moved in the bed; and I could smell the straw through the ticking. I was plagued by asthma attacks as a child and I really believe that straw prompted some of my most acute attacks. I kept the entire household up many nights with my coughing and wheezing. Mother and Daddy's room was right beside ours and in the really hot days of summer, Daddy would set a tiny oscillating fan on a stool in the doorway that adjoined the two rooms. I remember often gasping for breath on those sweltering nights. That little fan never moved much air, but I was really grateful when it sent some my way.

I remember getting a real mattress for our bed and thinking how wonderful it was; not having to smell all that straw. I don't think we had that new mattress very long before I christened it with a thorough soaking. I often wet the bed and would wake Roger complaining about the soggy mattress. He should have been the one complaining, but I don't ever remember him saying a word about it. Mama would have to bring a warm, dry towel to spread under my little wet butt to get me to go back to sleep.

I still recall to this day, a dream I had one night when I was around six or seven years old: *I was eating a watermelon while standing beside of one of Uncle Gordon's haystacks. When I finished eating the watermelon, I reared back and tried my best to pee all the way over the top of the haystack.* The dream appeared to be so real at the time. I found when I awoke, that one thing about it had actually happened—I really had been peeing. I think I just about washed Roger completely out of the bed that night. I still remember that dream after all these years and how real it seemed. I don't know to this day, why Roger didn't kill me before I was ten years old.

All three of us kids were still sleeping in the same room in the mid-1950s. By then, Laura was beginning to need a little privacy, so we added a bedroom; and living room to our little four room house. Mama wanted one of those big picture windows; that were in vogue at that time, to be installed in our living room.

We covered the entire house with asbestos siding when we added the new rooms. Daddy, "Bub" Rinehardt, Roger, Laura, Mama, and I built the rooms ourselves. I remember nailing the sub-floor, the outside walls, and the roof. That was one time that Daddy got some work out of me. Mama wanted the living room so that Laura would have a place to take her dates. However, I don't think she ever had a single date in that room. Most of the time, she and her date would sit in the swing on the front porch until they went to the movies or something. I was always in bed by the time they got home and I never saw them anyway.

Laura married Larry Neill on Christmas Eve in 1958, while she was still in high school, and I immediately claimed her bedroom as my own. I really enjoyed having my own room. The only problem was when I came home late at night—I had to go through Mama and Daddy's bedroom to get to mine. Daddy's side of the bed was right beside my bedroom door. I tried to be extremely quiet and not wake him, especially when I was late for my curfew. That endeavor was usually about as successful as trying to sneak dawn past a rooster. He always heard me—I never got away with anything.

**Our house in the 1980's**

I was allowed, for the first time, to ask someone to spend the night with me since I now had my own room. I remember Johnny Freeze spending the night on several occasions. He taught me to play the guitar and we double dated a lot.

I quickly developed an interest in music when I started playing the guitar and liked the early rock-and-roll and country songs the best. Johnny and I got pretty good playing together on some of the songs of the day. I only had a Sears Silvertone guitar at that time, but it played, nonetheless.

Mama had gotten rid of our old piano years before because we just didn't have room for it in the little four-room house. But, she was able to get another one after we added the new living room; and the house was once again filled with music. Mother loved to play the piano but all of the songs she played sounded about the same—I think she played them all in the same key.

When we children started our own families and began coming back home on Christmas mornings; the living room finally became a worthwhile addition to our house. Mama started setting the Christmas tree in front of the picture window that she had wanted so much. That new room provided a lot more space for all of us to gather around the tree and open our presents. Having all of us together made it a special time for Mama and Daddy.

We had many happy occasions in that room and some sad ones, too. Daddy passed away in July, 1970 and Mama brought him home to lie-in-state in the living room—the very room we all had built together. Mama passed away in 1995 and the house was sold to a nice young couple, Greg and Jane Fitchlee, who lovingly restored and remodeled both the interior and exterior. Vinyl siding and shutters now adorn the Ketchie house and it doesn't look like the same old place—it looks the best it's ever looked. I guess you might say that it has had an *"Extreme Makeover"*.

**Our house in 2006**

I am happy that the new owners have taken pride in our old house and made it a beautiful home.

# Radio and Television

Our family still had a four-room house in the early 1950's and there was an old upright piano in our living room that took up a lot of space. The blasted thing never seemed to stay in tune, so one day Mama traded it for a new Zenith AM/FM radio. Our old radio would only pick up AM stations and there was always a lot of static that interfered with our reception. That new FM model was really nice. The cabinet was made out of dark-brown plastic and had a big gold-colored circular dial on the front of it. I would almost drive Mama crazy; twisting the side-mounted knobs while she was trying to listen to it.

Mama always had that radio on while she was ironing and I would be playing on the floor in the kitchen with my cars and trucks listening along with her. I can still hear her as she sang along with Hank Williams when they played *Your Cheatin' Heart.* I still know the words to most of the old songs learned during those times I spent playing at Mama's feet.

Songs like: *It is no Secret, Goodnight Irene, Four Leaf Clover, I Saw the Light,* and many, many more come to mind. I often play the guitar with friends at Kenneth Overcash's house on Monday nights and we invariably end up singing some of the old-time favorites. We never know who is going to show up at his "pickin' shed", but we usually have about every kind of instrument necessary to play some lively tunes. Chuck Kyles has a fantastic voice and knows just about all the old standards. I think he sings *Fraulein* and *Goodnight Irene* better than the artists that recorded them. We really enjoy our times together on Monday nights playing those old favorites that never go out of style—we play a lot of Bluegrass, too.

You could always depend on the fact that breakfast at the Ketchie house rarely varied from its routine. We usually had mush and sausage, home-made biscuits, coffee, and the radio playing country music. I can still hear the announcer from WFMX in Statesville saying every morning as he signed off his portion of the program with: *"We'll be back tomorrow, same time, same station, the Good Lord willing, and the creeks don't rise, and the old buckboard holds together"*. I'll never forget those really good times spent around our breakfast table.

Many evenings would find our entire family listening to the radio together. Most nights we tuned in to the *Grand Ole Opry, Lum and Abner, The Phanthom, The Lone Ranger, Amos and Andy,* or *Perry Mason.* There were some really good shows on the radio in those days. I also liked *Jack Benny* and *George Burns and Gracie Allen,* too. They always made us laugh!

There were many sad announcements heard over our radio, too. Mama and Daddy heard President Franklin D. Roosevelt announce the invasion of Pearl Harbor and the declaration of war with Japan. I wasn't born when that took place, but I often heard them talking about it.

I do remember hearing a couple of historical events on the radio. I was listening when they announced that the last shots had been fired ending the Korean conflict. I didn't understand any of it, but I remember Mama was happy about it.

When I was working at Draymore Manufacturing Company, they played the radio over the intercom so everyone could listen to music while they worked. I will never forget the tragic day, when the announcer suddenly interrupted the broadcast and informed us that President John F. Kennedy had been shot, and asked us to stay tuned for more details. A little later, we learned that President Kennedy had died and a reverent silence fell over the entire plant. Hearing such earth-shattering events unfold as they were happening was quite a sobering experience for all of us. Those three days in November 1963 surely left an indelible impression on me.

Radio was a big thing in our house until we found out about this thing called television. Our lives were never the same after TV invaded our living room. We couldn't afford a television for our home until many years after all the neighbors had theirs.

Aunt Ruth Ketchie won a brand new television at the grand opening of the Medical Arts Pharmacy in the early 1950's, or they wouldn't have had a TV at Grandma's house, either. It was a 17" Emerson and I can still remember the day she brought it home. The entire Ketchie clan gathered round and watched Aunt Ruth with great anticipation as she plugged the TV's electrical cord into the receptacle. A pair of "rabbit ears" was attached and set on top of the television for better reception. All of us kids scattered around on the floor in front of the television set and were now officially ready to begin our life of TV addiction. I think Grandma and Aunt Ruth received a lot more visitors than normal after Aunt Ruth's good fortune.

Television stations didn't broadcast twenty-four hours a day then, like they do now. They signed on and off each day with the playing of the National Anthem. Before the broadcasts would begin, there would be a test-pattern on the screen for about an hour. I couldn't wait for the station to sign on in the morning and would sit there and just look at the profile of the big Indian chief on the test pattern. I thought that was pretty special even though the Indian never moved. It didn't take much to keep me entertained.

Aunt Ruth kept the television in what we called the "front room". There weren't many chairs in there so I would often have to lie on the floor while I watched television. There was an old, musty carpet on the floor that often caused me to have an asthma attack, and I would usually have to go home early.

I spent the night at Grandma Ketchie's as often as I could after they got that television. Aunt Ruth worked on the third shift at Cascade Mills and would often let me stay up and watch TV with her until she had to leave for work around 10:30 P.M. We didn't have a television set at our house yet, so to be able to watch hers was a real treat.

I tried to talk Mama into letting me to go to Grandma's every Saturday morning. I wanted to watch: *The Lone Ranger, Roy Rogers, Super Circus, The Big Top, Captain Midnight, Sky King, Superman,* and any old western movies that came on Aunt Ruth's new TV. Saturday was definitely a day for kids to watch television.

"Kawabonga, Buffalo Bob", I almost forgot about *The Howdy Doody Show* with Clarabell the clown and Chief Thunderthud, and of course the star, Howdy Doody. Buffalo Bob, dressed in buckskins, and his lovable freckled-face puppet Howdy Doody were the real stars of the show. They always played to a live audience of children seated in what was called the Peanut Gallery. *The Howdy Doody Show* ran for years and was one of the most beloved children's programs of the time.

There was usually a pretty good crowd of us grandchildren scattered around the front room every Saturday morning.

Watching television on Sunday was an entirely different story. For some reason, unbeknownst to us young people, there weren't any old western movies, circuses, or any of our favorite shows aired on Sundays. I thought they should have shown them everyday!

There was one show that I never really understood and that was *Omnibus.* Aunt Ruth tuned in often and claimed that just watching it would make me a smarter boy. I watched it with her anyway but couldn't tell much difference in my brain activity. I think *Omnibus* was for people that were already educated beyond their intelligence—I was a lost cause. *The Ed Sullivan Show* aired on Sunday nights and I liked that a lot. Ed Sullivan looked like he might have had his neck broken at one time because he couldn't turn his head very well—it didn't seem to bother him, though. He had a huge variety of acts on his show: comedians, circus performers, dancers, magicians, and singers. Ed seemed to take great pride introducing the celebrities in his audience. He must have given them free tickets, because there was always a bunch of them attending his shows.

We could only watch one station in the early days and that was WBTV, Channel 3, out of Charlotte. *Arthur Smith and the Cracker Jacks* seemed to have been a favorite of the older folks at Grandma's house. They really liked the variety of music and homespun humor that were featured on that show. Arthur Smith's brother, Ralph, and Tommy Faile played a comical pair of hillbilly cut-ups in their skit *Brother Ralph and Cousin Fudd.* Their hilarious antics would have everyone laughing—even Grandma. Another skit, *Counselors of the Airways,* was always one of our favorites. TV listeners would supposedly write to the counselors and ask for advice. Their answers would often be off-the-wall and never taken seriously. Don Reno was their banjo picker and played a character called *Chicken Hot Rod.* Don Reno was one of the best banjo pickers that I had ever seen in my few short years. He eventually formed his own band and went on to become a *Grand Ole Opry* star. Well, I guess I must have liked the *Cracker Jacks,* too—how else would I have remembered all of that stuff.

The networks introduced thirty-minute dramas that came on every day and catered to the stay-at-home housewives. Many women became addicted to them. Those programs later became known as "soap operas". Aunt Lib would set up her ironing board in the front room and I would often join her because she would invariably have some of her wonderful sugar cookies to assuage my hunger pains.

She watched *Search for Tomorrow* everyday. As far as I know, she never missed one episode. I wasn't even allowed to talk when it was on, but it was worth my silence just to have some of her cookies. I would usually last about half-way through one of the episodes (or until the cookies ran out) before I decided it was time to go outside and play.

There was also a big bookcase in the front room that was loaded with *National Geographic* magazines that belonged to Aunt Ruth. When nobody was watching television; Joe and I would sneak in there and look at the pictures of naked natives from Borneo or somewhere. Each magazine seemed to have a lot of pictures like that, or maybe we just kept looking at the same ones. We figured out a few things on our own about the female anatomy from those illuminating *National Geographic* magazines. It is truly amazing; the things young people had to do just to get an education.

I have a huge collection of *National Geographic* magazines today, upstairs at my gallery. They date all the way back to the 1920's—but, I don't look at them any more.

I remember the day that our family got its first television set. Daddy bought it from a man in Troutman named Kenneth Suther. We kids were so thrilled when Mr. Suther brought that big television into our home; we could have died right there. It was a huge thing that took up the entire corner of the den. The cabinet was humongous, but it only had a tiny twelve-inch screen. It was a Hallicrafters—a brand that I had never heard of before. It was used and a lot cheaper than a brand-name model like Zenith or RCA. Daddy wanted Mr. Suther to show him how to operate it, but Mr. Suther quickly explained that it would be best if he showed us kids, instead. He was right, too! There were no remote controls in those days and we were always the ones who had to get up and change the channels for Daddy anyway. He didn't like it too much when we would give that dial a fast whirl when we changed the channels. He thought that would really do harm to our television.

The very first show that I got to see on our new TV was *The Little Rascals.* A cowboy dressed to the nines, and strumming his guitar, introduced the episode where "Our Gang" was trying out for a talent contest to earn money for baseball equipment. The *Rascals* were calling themselves, something like, *The International Submarine String Band,* and of course, they won first place. I could hardly believe all the trouble they got into. They reminded me of us Ketchie kids.

Fred Kirby was that singing cowboy. He and his horse "Calico" were adored by children in the entire Charlotte viewing area. Jim Patterson, better known as "Uncle Jim" became his sidekick and together they led us kids through many happy hours of wholesome fun. Fred was known for his yodeling when he sang, *Take Me Back to My Boots and Saddle,* and other western standards. He also wrote and recorded a popular song entitled, *Atomic Power.* Fred loved children and frequently visited area hospitals and the Holy Angels Nursery in Belmont. Fred participated in and was the star of many parades around the Charlotte area.

Television became a very important part of my life. I soon found that when I was sick and not able to go to school, I could lie on the couch and watch TV. I even pretended I was sick occasionally so I could stay home and watch it. That only worked for a while before Daddy caught on. You couldn't fool Daddy too often and get away with it. There wasn't too much good stuff on during school days, anyway except, game shows. I soon learned that playing hooky wasn't worth the trouble.

Our family often watched TV together after the supper dishes were done. Perry Mason was one of the most popular shows at our house. Perry was a famous big-city lawyer known for winning all of his cases, sometimes against all odds. The district attorney, Hamilton Berger and homicide, detective Lieutenant Tragg were always determined to prosecute Perry's clients. Daddy would tell us each week that Perry was going to lose his case, so we couldn't wait to see if that would really happen. I don't remember him ever losing a case. Perry Mason was a cool dude if there ever was one.

Another favorite of the entire family was *Amos and Andy*. I just loved watching Kingfish Stevens trying to get the best of poor, unsuspecting Andy Brown.

Daddy would laugh until he cried watching Lucille Ball play Lucy Ricardo in *I Love Lucy*. You never knew what kind of mess Lucy, and her side-kick Ethel Mertz, would get into next. Lucy's husband, Ricky, was the band leader at the Tropicana Night Club and she desperately wanted to perform in one of the acts at his club. Lucy would resort to about anything to make it happen, even though she was not very talented. Her zany antics are timeless and continue to entertain us today on the cable channel TVLand.

I was in the seventh grade when The Real McCoys aired for the first time. Walter Brennan starred as Grandpa Amos McCoy, the patriarch of the family. Richard Crenna played his son Luke, and together with his wife Kate, daughter Hassie, and son Little Luke, lived with Grandpa on a small farm. The McCoys were country people just like us. It seemed that everybody else on television was always dressed up and lived in fine houses in town. *Ozzie and Harriet* and *Leave it to Beaver* were prime examples of what I thought the average American family was supposed to be like. We surely didn't live like they did. We were more like the McCoy family.

1960 brought to our living rooms, one of the all-time best loved shows that television ever produced. It is still enjoyed by fans around the world everyday. Even though I have probably seen each episode a dozen times, I don't miss an opportunity to watch a rerun of *The Andy Griffith Show*. Andy Griffith plays Andy Taylor, a small town sheriff, with Don Knotts portraying his bumbling deputy, Barney Fife. Andy's Aunt Bee lives with him and his son Opie. The cast is rounded out with some great supporting characters that include: Floyd the barber, Otis the town drunk, the laughable Gomer Pyle, and his cousin Goober, and we could never forget Ernest T. Bass. Ernest T.'s bread isn't quite done but he is hilarious. Opie's school teacher, Mrs. Crump, and Andy finally get married, but poor ole Barney and his girl, Thelma Lou never quite get it together. I suppose I like *The Andy Griffith Show* better than anything else that the television industry has offered in the last forty years.

Television not only entertained us and made us laugh, but informed us about current events. Daddy watched the evening news every night and kept up with what was going on in the world.

I will never forget watching television with Daddy as the venerable Walter Kronkite described the very moment that man first landed on the moon. We were both apprehensive as we witnessed Neill Armstrong take the historic, first step on lunar soil. I remember looking at Daddy and seeing him wiping tears from his eyes with his handkerchief. We had just shared an enormous event in the history of the entire world. That was July 20 1969. I am extremely grateful to have shared that moment with my father—he passed away less than a year later.

I remember not having a television when Jean and I first got married in 1963. We finally bought one for seventy dollars from Harry Keeter at Besk's Jewelers. He let us pay for it in installments or we could have never owned one. It was only a little table model and we had to set it up on a shelf over the refrigerator to watch it.

Vickie and I married in 1987 and her youngest son, Darrin, came in the house one day so excited that he could hardly stand it. He had just returned home from watching television at a friend's house.

He said, "Mama, you're not going to believe this."

"Believe what?" Vickie asked.

"They had a television that doesn't play anything but "black-and-white." Darrin was really impressed. He was not born until March of 1984 and had only seen color television.

Vickie and I got a good laugh out of that observation. It's hard to believe all the things that have been invented since I was born over sixty years ago.

# Fun and Games

Daddy was always fun-loving and would make lots of things for us to play with that required using our imaginations. A discarded hoop from an old nail keg and a stick with a crosspiece Daddy had nailed to the bottom, would entertain me for hours. I would push the hoop along with the stick and go all the way to Grandma's house and back without letting it fall over. That was quite an accomplishment for a little boy. At least, I thought it was.

I remember when Daddy made us some stilts, (We called them "Tommy Walkers".) He nailed two blocks of wood to some two-by-twos to make steps for our feet. We would climb up on them, hold on to the two-by-twos and walk across the yard—two feet taller than before. They were great fun and we thought we were really something special because we towered above everyone else when we walked on them. Roger and Laura were much better at walking on those stilts than I was.

One summer, Daddy cut down a weeping willow tree that stood in our backyard. He left the stump just about waist high and sawed the top off to make it completely level. Then, he greased the top of the stump with axle grease. Next, Daddy drilled a hole through the middle of a two-by-eight piece of lumber and bolted it to the stump. He screwed a board to each end of the two-by-eight so we would have something to hook our legs over and get a handhold. We didn't know what he had in mind for this contraption, but we watched with great curiosity as it was coming to fruition.

Daddy christened his invention the Merry-Go-Round, and Laura and I were summarily put astride each end of the big board. We were instructed to hook our legs over the crosspiece and grab hold of it with our hands. Daddy asked us if we were ready and started spinning the Merry-Go-Round as hard as he could. The next thing I knew, we were flying round and round as fast as Daddy could keep that thing spinning. I saw our house, the shop, Mr. Malcolm's house, Roger, Daddy, and Mother—all at one time. I was holding on as hard as I could, and Laura was screaming bloody murder. I laughed so hard I wet my pants. I had never experienced anything like that before. What a ride! I never knew what it was like to be drunk, but after that, I had a pretty good idea. The Merry-Go-Round became the focal point for the entire neighborhood. Everyone came to give it a whirl. We had a ton of fun on that thing, and it will live in my memory forever.

**With Laura on the Merry-Go-Round**

One summer, Daddy went down to Uncle Frank's pasture and cut some willow branches from the creek bank. Using these branches, he meticulously made a replica of my great-grandfather, Noah Ketchie's home-place, complete with an old well, corn crib, and other out-buildings. The front porch roof is gone from the main house, but I still have the entire set.

**The old Ketchie place made out of willow branches**

I was in the first or second grade at Shepherd School when an older boy, Arnold Clark, taught me how to make a really good paper airplane. I had always made the long, skinny ones that would just go straight and quickly crash before flying ten feet. Arnold got down on his hands and knees and patiently showed me how to fold my notebook paper to make this super flying airplane. I would throw it in the air, and if it caught a breeze, it would stay up for a long, long time. One day, one of these fantastic-flying planes I made was caught by a gentle wind and kept going and going until it landed on the roof of Shepherd School. When the teachers were not looking, Arnold climbed up on the roof and got it down for me. I have made some of those paper airplanes for my children to fly and now I am making them for my grandchildren. It's hard to believe that it has been over fifty years since I learned to make those planes.

I always liked airplanes and thought they were some of the most beautiful man-made objects in existence. I had a big, toy airplane made out of metal with real rubber wheels that were connected to the propellers by small cables. The propellers would go round and round when you rolled it across the ground.

**My toy airplane**

That airplane was so special I was afraid to let anyone else play with it very much. Doggone, it was beautiful! I still have the plane today, but the propellers won't go round and round any more. That plane is just about as old as I am—but it's in better condition.

I started putting model airplanes together as I grew older. I remember saving my money so I could begin a collection of plastic airplane models. Some of my friends were collecting them, so I thought that I should too. I had all kinds of models. My favorites were the P-51 Mustang, the F-104-A Starfighter, the P-40 Flying Tiger, and the P-47D

Thunderbolt. I liked them all! I had a few model boats, too. The graceful lines of the airplanes and boats always intrigued me. To me, they were truly works of art that I could hold in my hands. I felt I had created something beautiful just by putting one of the models together. I still have a couple of them upstairs at my gallery. Some have missing parts and some are broken, but I just can't make myself part with any of them. I never know when I might need a model of a P-47D Thunderbolt—if the need ever arises, I'll have one.

I enjoyed playing with my toy cars and trucks as much as anything. Of course, I was really young and had not yet been included in some of Roger's adventures.

We didn't have much grass growing in our yard near the back of our house, and that was a great place to make roads through the dirt with Daddy's hoes. He had a regular hoe, used for hoeing the garden and chopping cotton, and he had a big, wide hoe that had two holes through it that was used for mixing mortar. I guess you could call it a mortar hoe. I used the big, wide one for making major highways through my make-believe town. The regular hoe was used for secondary roads.

One year, I got a toy, metal, service station for Christmas. I thought that it was the "cat's meow". I set the station in amongst the roads of my little "town" so that my cars and trucks could drive right up to the station and fill up with gas. I don't have the service station anymore. One time I got curious and tried to figure out how it was put together. Taking it apart was easy, but I bent the metal tabs so badly that they wouldn't hold the roof on or the sides up any longer. I guess I should have learned how to weld!

Aunt Margaret and Uncle Tom Brantley gave me a great big, metal, dump truck that had "SAND" written on one side of the bed and "GRAVEL" on the other side. The cab was royal blue and the bed of the truck was a bright red. I played with that truck until I wore it slap out.

I also had a big, bright-yellow car that was made of out of plastic. It had a big hole in the center of the back where sparks would fly out when you raced it along. It was sleek and modern and reminded me of a jet airplane. I finally ran the wheels off that yellow car.

Sometimes, Laura would join me, and we would crawl around on our knees while driving our vehicles along the winding, sandy roads. It was really special when Daddy would get a load of sand for laying bricks. He would have to use it pretty fast, or we would have it scattered "six ways from Sunday" all over our little town.

All of us kids liked to play marbles and would often draw a ring in the sand behind the back door of our house and shoot marbles all day long. One marble game was called Pig Eye. The shooting area was in the shape of a small half-circle instead of a ring like we used for regular marble games. It looked kind of like a "pig's eye", hence the name. The marbles were put into the pig's eye and a line was drawn in the sand about two feet from the half-circle. You had to shoot from behind that line all the way into the half circle to hit the marbles and hopefully knock some of them out of the ring. The ones you knocked out were yours to keep. Needless to say, I was not very adept at those long shots that were needed to win many marbles. I don't think that I ever beat anyone in Pig Eye.

More often than not, we shot regular marbles at Shepherd School. We drew a ring about three feet in diameter and everyone put their marbles into the ring. Every player knew which marbles were theirs and each one tried to shoot their opponent's marbles out of the ring. It was a thrill to knock two or three of them out with one shot. You kept all the marbles you knocked out of the circle in the course of a game. I had a big steel marble one time, and it would knock the fire out of their little "aggies". I even had a marble made out of clay. We called it a "pee-dab". It wasn't worth "Jack Squat". It was too light to knock anybody's marble out of the ring. Those "pee-dabs" were good to have in the ring if you didn't want to lose your best marbles. Sometimes, but not very often, I could find somebody willing to shoot marbles just for fun.

Two girls at school would just about "clean my clock" every time I shot marbles with them. They were the Smith twins, Sue and Sybil, two of the best marble shooters in all of Shepherd School. They only played for keeps, too; they never played just for fun. I lost a ton of marbles to those girls. Sue and Sybil were Laura's age and should have had some sympathy for a little boy that was three years younger than they were. The Smith twins never took any prisoners— they just took your marbles. They never got all of mine though. I still have a big jar of them.

Mama was constantly patching my jeans. I kept them worn out from crawling on my knees all the time, shooting marbles or playing with my cars and trucks.

Laura and I were tricycle buddies. You may notice who rode the nicer one that had the fender. The front wheel on mine kept wobbling and trying to fall off, but I persevered, being the stalwart young boy that I was.

**Laura and me on our favorite tricycles**

She was the one who taught me to ride a bicycle. That was no easy task because I was extremely athletically challenged. We didn't have a girl's bicycle, and Laura wasn't big enough to straddle the bar on Roger's bike; so she would stick her leg through the bars to reach the other pedal. It never slowed her down—she could ride circles around us.

When three country kids were looking for something to do on a warm summer day—trouble was usually not far behind. I, being the youngest and the least worldly was highly susceptible to any suggestion from my older siblings. I usually did just about anything they asked because I always wanted to be included in the fun.

Well, one, so far uneventful, morning was slowly dragging on when a big truck from Duke Power Company pulled up in front of our house and stopped. We couldn't wait to see what they were going to do next.

We watched with great anticipation as the workers disembarked from their vehicle and promptly started digging a large hole in our front yard with these extremely long-handled post-hole diggers. When the hole was completed, it looked to me like it was six to eight feet deep and about two feet wide. Then, a huge utility pole was unloaded and placed beside the hole.

Twelve o'clock arrived and the men from Duke Power were leaving for lunch and leaving us three Ketchie kids staring in awe at the huge hole in our front yard. We were politely asked to not let anyone near the edge of the hole for fear that someone might fall in it while they were at lunch.

Well, it didn't take very long for Roger to conjure up one of his great ideas for having fun. I was hastily elected by the majority of the Ketchie kids that were present, to be the one who would have a rope tied around his waist and lowered into the freshly dug hole.

Laura, always willing to help, found a stout piece of rope and Roger quickly tied it around me before I could change my mind. As I was eased down to the very bottom of the hole, I looked skyward into the happy faces of my brother and sister and wondered to myself; how in the world I let them talk me into this.

I could hear them in conversation with someone at ground level but I couldn't hear exactly what was being said. I was pretty sure that it was not going to be very encouraging, whatever it was. Well, good old Mr. Malcolm from next door had been watching as the misadventures of the Ketchie kids were unfolding before his eyes. He could have stopped the entire exercise in foolhardiness at anytime, but chose not to do so.

Mr. Malcolm had quite a reputation in the Shepherd's Community for stretching the truth to fit the situation. He never passed up an opportunity to try one of his dubious stories on us gullible kids. He peered down into the dark hole where I was imprisoned and told us that Duke Power had just put a utility pole right smack-dab on top of a little boy who was in one of their freshly dug holes. To make matters worse—it happened right up the road—and they were coming to our house next!

The prospect of being the next smashed little boy didn't set too well with me. I commenced to hollering so loud that Mr. Malcolm retreated to the quieter confines of his house. Roger and Laura kept peering over the edge of the hole, trying to get me to calm down before Daddy heard all the commotion and came to see what was going on. I think that my hollering hastened my rescue considerably.

When the men from Duke Power returned to our house from their lunch break, we were all seated on the big utility pole as if nothing had ever happened. They even thanked us for standing guard and making sure that nobody fell into the hole.

We were not about to tell them the truth. We stayed to oversee the entire operation of utility-pole-planting. I was just thankful that I was no longer confined to the depths of that deep, dark hole. I shuddered when I heard the muffled "kathunk", as the pole hit the bottom of the earthen abyss and a cloud of red dust rose slowly to meet the summer sky.

After the pole was set and dirt packed firmly around it, I started breathing a little easier. Then, we went to the backyard in search of less stressful adventures.

I still have the jack-in–the-box that I have had since I was five or six years old. When I cranked the handle on the side, it played *Pop Goes the Weasel* and the top would fly up and make a clown jump out at you. I loved that toy! I think that the weasel-popping thing is broken now, but it still looks good. I believe it is still worth keeping for a few more decades.

I bought a Slinky for myself when they were the rage. I would take it to Grandma's house and make it go down the stairs, one step at a time. That thing amazed me; I don't know why I couldn't have invented something like that. My daddy always said that I would find a way to make a living besides working for it. I'm still trying!

I also had a Hula-Hoop. It was one of the biggest fads that ever hit the country in the late 1950's. Watching Mama trying to keep that Hula-Hoop going reminded me of an old comedy act that I used to see on *The Ed Sullivan Show*. She wasn't too coordinated, and the moves she put on that thing were hilarious. I couldn't Hula-Hoop much better than Mama and probably looked just as silly. Mama and I were a lot alike; it was difficult for us to walk and chew gum at the same time. I guess I was quite a lazy youngster, and it took way too much of my energy to stand there and swivel my hips. I was born tired and didn't want to waste any of the little energy I had doing something like that. However, I didn't mind bending my elbow while transporting food to my mouth.

We loved putting jigsaw puzzles together in the winter months. It was hard to get us to do any work when we had a major puzzle project going. I remember one incident when Mama had asked us numerous times to do a certain chore; and somehow, it just didn't get done. That was evidently the last straw for her. (She had a lot of last straws.) Mama came in the room where we were putting the puzzle together and raked all the pieces into the box. We had seen her do that before, but we were slow learners. This time, she took our puzzle (box and all), opened the stove door, and threw the whole thing into the fire. I couldn't believe it! Before anybody could think, Roger jumped up and stuck his hand in the fire and retrieved our favorite puzzle. Some of the pieces were scorched a little bit around the edges, but that just helped us find where they fit together easier.

One of our favorite games was called Finance. It was a board game that was played a lot like Monopoly. We also played a lot of checkers and Chinese checkers. I still have those board games upstairs in my gallery for safekeeping.

One time, Daddy cut a square board from a piece of plywood, rounded off the corners, and drilled indentations in it at strategic places. These indentations held marbles as they were moved around the board. Every player had a cup that held their dice, and would roll them to see where to move their marbles. You could kill some unfortunate player's marble, and he would have to start that one all over again. When one player got all six of his marbles home, safe and sound, he was declared the winner. It was a fast-action game that was enjoyed by our entire family. We called the game "Crazy Marbles".

My first (serious) girlfriend, Fazelle Henderson, liked to play the game with us. She came to our house often and joined in a lot of the Ketchie games. (See picture on next page.) Daddy was highly competitive, but took losing in his usual graceful manner. Roger usually took losing pretty well too, but Mama sometimes took losing personally. She would get really excited and take umbrage with anyone who would have the audacity to land on one of her marbles and send it back to start all over again. I was a lot like my mama. (I didn't like to lose too much either.)

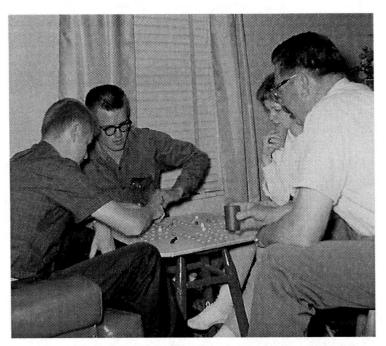

**"Crazy Marbles" with Roger, Fazelle, and Daddy"**

I had a wonderful childhood with great parents that patiently nurtured me through my adolescent years. They also had fun with us, and I think that is one of the most important things they did.

# A Christmas Dream

Christmas was always a magical time for me when I was a child growing up in the country. Daddy was unable to work regularly and Mother eventually went to work at one of the cotton mills in Mooresville. No one in our family ever had much money. We were not <u>extremely</u> poor, but we were really close to being severely middle-classed. Nonetheless, we always seem to have a memorable Christmas.

I looked forward to that special day of Christmas with so much anticipation I could barely sleep from Thanksgiving Day to December the 24th. December is the longest month of the year for young children. If you don't believe it, just ask one.

The idea of a jolly, old man in a red suit who would personally visit our home each year to bring us presents was just hard for me to comprehend. I really had trouble with the idea of Santa coming down our chimney—we had a wood stove, for gosh sakes! I was worried that he wouldn't come to see us at all.

Because Roger and Laura were a lot older than I was, I thought they knew just about everything. I suppose that my cousin, Joe, would rank right up there with them. He and Roger were in the same grade at Shepherd School. They told me how Santa would come and bring all the stuff that I asked him to bring me for Christmas if I would just be a good boy all year long. I doubted I had a chance, but I dreamed anyway. The biggest and best thing I could hope for would be an Erector Set or a Daisy Red Ryder BB Gun. What more could a boy of nine years of age ever hope to get for Christmas?

Christmas Eve finally arrived and Aunt Sarah, Aunt Ruth, Aunt Catherine, and all my cousins, along with our family, met at Grandma's and gathered around the big wood-stove in the parlor. It was a family tradition.

Each year, sometime before Christmas, we drew names so we could exchange gifts. This one special year stands out in my mind because it was the first time I was allowed to participate in the name drawing with the adults. I had been doing every kind of chore I could think of and saving my money to buy a present for the person whose name I was going to draw. I was excited because I was the lucky one who drew Grandma's name out of Uncle Gordon's hat. I bought her a navy-blue sweater-coat, the kind she liked to wear all winter.

The time finally came for opening presents, and I got a pair of real leather gloves. They were the first pair that I had ever owned and I couldn't wait to try them out. I put them on right then, and wore them the rest of the evening. Grandma was the last one to open her present, and everybody was trying to figure out who had drawn her name. It was worse than having your teeth pulled, just watching and waiting for her to finally get the doggoned paper off the present. She carefully took the tape loose at each end of the box. Then she took the paper and folded it up, real neat, so she could use it again to wrap someone else's present. I would have ripped that thing open so fast it would have made your head swim. Not her; she made this moment really last, and the suspense in the room grew thick with anticipation. I think she had already figured out who had drawn her name and was giving me my moment of glory. She took the lid off the box and announced to the crowd that had gathered around her, "Guess who drew my name?"

I was so excited to be the center of attention I grinned like a possum. Grandma really loved her sweater, and everyone was surprised that I had saved enough money to buy her such a nice gift—Daddy probably helped me with some of the financing. I think the sweater cost four dollars.

As time slowly ticked off the clock, Daddy finally said, "Why don't we take a drive into town and look at the Christmas lights?" We kids jumped all over that idea with enthusiasm. We piled in our 1950, two-door Plymouth and rode all over Mooresville, oohing and aahing at the beautiful holiday decorations that "well off" people had. We rode down Cedar Street and all over the "Mill Hill". The Mill Hill was actually the village that was built around the old cotton mill that was located on South Main Street. The mill, itself, always had pretty lights, too, as did the downtown area. It was really exciting for us country kids to see all those brightly colored lights.

All we had at our house was just a regular, old-fashioned, cedar tree that we had cut down in the pasture behind Grandma's. It took much thought and planning to find a tree that would please all of us kids. (We usually didn't agree on too much stuff.)

Roger was the designated tree cutter because he was the oldest. We would take turns carrying it back to the house. A discarded piece of plywood was nailed to the bottom of the tree after the trunk had been evenly sawed off. Years later, Mama bought one of those stands that you could keep water in so the tree didn't dry out too quickly. She was always the one who was up on the latest inventions. I suppose you could say she was better informed than we were. The rest of us didn't give a rat's hat; all we wanted was a tree with pretty lights.

We covered the tree with tin foil icicles, a few glass ornaments, some silver garland, and multi-colored lights. The lights were those great big, bulbs that would burn the fire out of you when you touched them. God was surely good and watched over us; He never let one of those highly flammable cedars, with those extremely hot lights draped all over it, catch fire. We were really proud of the way our homegrown tree looked in front of the window.

We had a little nativity scene, too; and it always filled me with wonder; seeing the little baby Jesus lying in the manger. I remember having a songbook with all the traditional Christmas carols. We gathered around Mama as she played our old out-of-tune piano and sang the carols with gusto—not very well, but with gusto. Daddy read the Christmas story, Luke 2: 8-20, from the Bible before we went to bed and all seemed well with the world.

Mama always made a coconut cake for Christmas. It was so moist it would almost melt in my mouth. I recall leaving a huge piece of that cake on a plate, accompanied by a six-ounce bottle of Coke, beside Daddy's chair on Christmas Eve for Santa Claus. I was told that it would give him energy so he could finish his Christmas rounds and would let him know how much we loved him.

It was so difficult for us children to go to sleep that Mother gave us some aspirin to help calm us down enough so that sleep could eventually overtake the anticipation. That night, before we went to sleep, I remember telling Roger that I heard a bump coming from the front of the house and thought it might be Santa Claus. I had already been informed by a reliable source that Santa had to come through our front door; because we had a wood-stove, and not a fireplace. I was really grateful that Santa Claus was an adaptable man. Well, Roger gave me the wise counsel of his fourteen years and assured me that it was not Santa, but just some of those familiar night-sounds that we often heard in our house. I believed him, of course, and finally went to sleep.

Sometime, really early in the morning, I awoke with a start, sensing that something was different. I felt that something magical had taken place, and I had slept right through the whole thing. I thought that waking up my sleeping brother and sister would be the wise thing to do. I had always heard that Santa came around midnight. I thought there was a chance he might be running a little late, and I didn't want to risk bumping into him, by myself. I was afraid he wouldn't appreciate anyone messing up his surprise, and I definitely didn't want to upset "The Man" on Christmas Eve.

I finally convinced Roger and Laura to get up and open the door to the front room where the Christmas tree was located. Seeing the big, silly grins on their faces assured me that Santa Claus had definitely come. I raced by them in a flash and hurried toward the tree. It didn't take me long to find an Erector Set and a Daisy Red Ryder BB Gun. I didn't know what Santa Claus had brought the rest of them; but I knew, without a shadow of a doubt, that the Red Ryder BB Gun belonged to nobody but me. There was also a pair of cotton gloves with the fringe hanging off the cuffs of them. They were just like the ones Red Ryder wore himself. I had been reading about Red Ryder and Little Beaver in comic books for a while and had seen them on Aunt Ruth's television. Every boy I knew had a Red Ryder BB gun and now I would, too. I thought I would die right there.

I was so excited that I almost forgot to check my stocking that Daddy had nailed to the mantle. It was crammed full with nuts, oranges, hard candy, and a few pieces of that wonderful stick candy. Some pieces of that hard candy were stuck to the felt in my stocking, but that never stopped me from eating it. We called the hard candy "Hard Rock Charlie". I never knew why we did that, but it always had that name in our family. I would usually cut a hole in my orange, stick a peppermint stick down into the hole, and suck the tangy juice up through the candy until the orange was dry. Then, I would tear it in half, and eat everything but the rind. We didn't get oranges except at Christmastime and they were always a special treat.

Daddy and Mother came drowsily into the living room to see why we were up so early. (Yeah, right!) They were quick to point out that Santa devoured the cake and drank the Coke. Daddy had this satisfied look on his face and some crumbs around his mouth. That always made me a little suspicious.

I found out, very sadly, that the Erector Set was too complicated for me, and I was talked into trading it with Roger for a pitiful, little box of metal puzzles. The puzzles weren't very challenging for Roger, and the Erector Set was too complicated for me—so things worked out pretty well for both of us.

I think this was the same year that Laura got her little, metal tea set. To this day, I remember playing House with her that next spring. (She made me do that a lot.) She would pour Nehi Grape Soda into one of the teacups and serve it to me. Then she would make me drink it while holding my little finger up in the air like dignified folks. I will never forget the taste of the rust from that little, tin cup mixed with the Nehi Grape Soda. Sometimes I think I can still taste the rust by just looking at a grape soda.

Each year, Roger, Laura, and I would pool our resources and buy Daddy at least three or four of those highly stinking El Moro Cigars. We had to get them from Mooresville Drug Store, at the corner of Main Street and Iredell Avenue. That was the only place we could find them. Mr. Charlie Crowell always helped us get the cigars for Daddy and knew that we kids weren't going to smoke those nasty things. They were the only kind of cigar that Daddy liked to smoke. Thank the good Lord that he only got three or four of the vile smelling things each year. I don't think Mama really appreciated all the thought that went in to buying Daddy those cigars. She couldn't stand to smell them, but we bought them every year for him, anyway.

I don't really remember what we bought Mama for Christmas each year; I think we often gave her some dish towels or some kind of "what not". Daddy had cut a big hole in the living room wall and made her specially designed shelves just to display her little, Japanese figurines. She had so many of those little things we had to dust on a regular basis; that our enthusiasm for buying them was somewhat tainted with reluctance; but we bought them for her, anyway. Daddy and Mama seemed pleased with their gifts, so everything worked out pretty well.

Every Christmas morning, we had a big breakfast that consisted of cornmeal mush, sausage, and homemade biscuits. Thinking about it later, we had mush and sausage almost every other day, too, but it just seemed more special

51

on Christmas. I remember about 5:30 on Christmas morning, Joe came busting through our back door as we were eating breakfast, carrying a real guitar that Santa had brought him. I was really impressed—to say the least. Joe couldn't even play the guitar yet, but he was a happy boy, and so were we.

I went outside before daylight and started shooting my new Red Ryder BB gun with as much pleasure a nine-year old country boy could muster. Once in a while, I could even hear a BB hitting something.

Christmas came and went that year, fulfilling my Christmas dreams of a BB gun, candy, nuts, fruit, and a loving family. What more could anyone ever hope for or deserve?

I kept that BB gun for many years and treasure the memories of childhood Christmases to this day. Even after all of us children were married, Daddy would call us every Christmas morning about 4:30 and want to know when we were going to be there—the mush had been on for hours. My parents' love for giving was handed down to each of us to pass along to our children.

Christmas has not been the same since Daddy and Mama passed away. Perhaps they are up there in Heaven, watching with pleasure as our children gather around the tree on Christmas morning, tearing paper from packages and squealing with delight.

I wish I knew where my genuine, Daisy Red Ryder BB Gun is today. And you know I actually miss that mush!

# Camping Out and Berry Picking

Camping out in the pasture behind Grandma's house is one of my fondest memories. My brother, Roger; my first cousin, Joe; neighbors, David and Jimmy Wilson; and I would often, literally, sleep out under the stars.

It is still hard for me to imagine that those teenage boys would let some kid that was five years younger than they were, tag along with them. I will always be indebted to them for their patience and generosity. About half the time, I would have an asthma attack, and Roger would have to walk me back home in the middle of the night and wake everybody up. Still, they put up with me.

To be included in such grand plans was like going on a huge adventure for me. Often, I would be made to do different chores like totin' and fetchin'. Usually these were the ones the big boys didn't want to do themselves. I was pretty young to have even been included; so I did the assigned tasks with as much enthusiasm as I could muster.

After the evening milking was done, we would load everything we could carry and trek down the old lane to the pasture before it got too dark. It was easier for me to carry things when they were strapped on my back so I would pack Daddy's old Army musette bag to carry some of my stuff.

We rarely slept in a tent. Sometimes, Daddy would loan us his little Army pup tent that was left over from World War II. It only had room for one; so each of us usually did without so that nobody would have special privileges. Most of the time, we put our supplies and food inside the tent in case it rained.

Daddy would often let us use his Army sleeping bag, too. Smelling that musty thing would just about guarantee that I would have an asthma attack—I usually let one of the other boys sleep in it. We usually just slept on the ground rolled up in old quilts or Daddy's Army blanket.

**Daddy, me, and the pup tent**

There was much to be done before we could even get a fire lit: the tent had to be set up, wood had to be gathered, and more often than not, someone had to run back to the house to get something that had been forgotten. I think the "running back to the house part" is one of the reasons I was allowed to go along in the first place. Whatever the reason, it was surely worth it. However, I didn't like to run back to the house by myself, after dark. It wasn't the dark that scared me; it was the things that I couldn't see that bothered me the most.

A big fire was always at the center of the campsite to ward off any unwanted varmints and was used to cook our meager meals. Big rocks were gathered to place around the fire for safety. I stayed near that fire; you never knew what evil lurked outside the range of the firelight! Water was dipped out of the small branch near our campsite to make coffee. The fact that we are still living is a testament to the importance of boiling water. Uncle Gordon's cows drank from the same stream we did, and Heaven knows what else they did while they were standing in that water. Nevertheless, I don't ever remember getting sick from drinking out of that branch.

Sometimes we would boil a concoction of water, grass, leaves, sticks, berries, and anything else that someone would dare to put in an old can. Then, we would see who was crazy enough to taste it. One time, I slipped a little bit of a cow pie in the can when nobody was looking, just to see what would happen. The stuff was so nasty anyway, nobody knew the difference. David Wilson always seemed to be the one who was up to the challenge and would try just about anything. He never got sick after drinking a little bit of it, but sometimes he would act a little funny.

One night, Joe and I camped out by ourselves and were making coffee in our old, camp-type coffeepot. We tied some coffee grounds into a small pouch, made out of a scrap of cloth, and put it down in the water. We kept wondering if and when it would ever be ready. We never smelled the coffee brewing; so we just kept waiting. Finally, Joe peeked in the pot to see what was going on, only to find that all the water had boiled away and our little sack of coffee had caught fire. We sneaked back to the house about 2:00 in the morning to get some more coffee and try again. We never claimed to be mental giants.

One memorable morning before daylight, I felt something like sandpaper raking across the side of my face. I thought I was dreaming. Having only a blanket to wrap up in, we never got much sleep on the cold ground anyway; so I was not really sure what was happening. It brought me wide awake to find out the raking was coming from the big, wet tongue of one of Uncle Gordon's milk cows. It didn't take much of that slobbering tongue to bring me out of my blanket! The rest of the guys thought the incident was hilarious, but it scared the "wahzoo" out of me.

We would all have to gather wood for the morning fire because we usually burned all we had during the night. We needed to cook breakfast in a hurry because we were usually starving. We always seemed to have overly stimulated appetites. Streak-of-Lean (bacon to city folks), a dozen or so eggs, some toast cooked on a stick held near the fire, and some of that awful coffee would make a terrific meal for us hungry boys. Sometimes, Aunt Lib would send some of her fantastic sugar cookies with us to devour while camping out. We would just about fight over those things.

Speaking of Aunt Lib's cookies, I am reminded of one occasion when I hid in Grandma's huge cupboard that ran along the entire kitchen wall behind the woodstove. A flour sack full of Aunt Lib's sugar cookies was kept there for safekeeping from predators like me. I already had a reputation for devouring copious amounts of sweets. I liked three kinds of food when I was young: sweet, sweet, and sweet! Well, I found out where the "cookie stash" was hidden, crawled inside, and silently closed the cupboard door. Everyone thought I was lost or had run away from home. I could hear everybody calling for me, but I wasn't about to answer until I had eaten all the cookies I could stuff down my throat. I probably ate fifty or more. I was only around six or seven years old at the time—my appetite hadn't fully developed yet. I did get a memorable whipping for my lapse in good judgment, but it was definitely worth it. It was the first and last time I ever pulled off the nefarious cookie-stealing stunt.

Getting back to camping out with the boys—Roger had a pouch of RJR smoking tobacco with him one night. Of course, we all had to test our adulthood by smoking some in a corncob pipe that he had bought in a souvenir shop in Cherokee. I remember asking Roger what RJR stood for, and he replied that it meant Run Johnny Run. Naturally, I believed him—he being the all-knowing big brother. How was I to know that RJR stood for the R.J. Reynolds Tobacco

Company? We had watched the grownups smoke for years and thought we would give it a try.

We also tried smoking corn silk, rabbit tobacco, and grapevines when we couldn't get our hands on some real tobacco. After we got the smoking habit, we even salvaged some cigarette butts from Daddy's ashtray. He smoked Camels and they were a little strong for us—but we smoked them anyway. The butts were always really short and we would sometimes singe our eyebrows when we tried to light one. We found out that smoking wasn't all that it was cracked up to be and quit when we got older.

One summer night while camping, we took the lantern and set it at the edge of the branch where the bank was about eight or ten feet above the streambed. The old, kerosene lantern was to be the target. The idea was to see who could get the closest to it without hitting it and knocking our only source of light into the water. This feat was to be attempted while racing down the hill in the dark on a three-wheeled car that Roger had made. We didn't know what we would run into—or over—on the way down the hill. Cow pies were plentiful and it was really bad news when we ran over a fresh one while riding that little car. It didn't have any fenders—if you get my drift. It was usually impossible to avoid them in the dark while flying down that hill; it took all we could do to just hold on and not fall off the doggoned car. God was good to us and let us escape unharmed from many of our hair-brained adventures.

Perhaps the most fun was having the older boys climb a tall tree and swing it down to the ground so one of us could ride it back up. Sometimes it would take two of them to provide enough weight to accomplish this brave task. I, being five years younger, was usually unanimously elected to be the one who was to wrap his arms and legs around the top of the tree and be launched into space. The big boys would let go on the count of ten and I would be catapulted, some times twenty or thirty feet in the air, while praying and holding on for dear life. The trick was not to let go—no matter what! I would have to wait for the tree to stop swaying back and forth and then find a way back down that once subdued tree to the safety of the blessed ground. That was a lot of fun but a little bit scary when I was the one doing the riding. This feat was always carried out while it was daylight. We weren't crazy enough to try that in the dark.

Sometimes we would go all the way down Uncle Frank Ketchie's lane and camp beneath a huge rock that projected out from a hill and over the pasture. At its base meandered a larger stream that we dammed up in the summer to make a pond for swimming. This same stream began at a big rock in the pinewoods behind Grandma's house and would lazily flow all the way to the Catawba River. However, we claimed this part of the stream to be ours.

In the summertime, the big meadow near that stream would be loaded with blackberries. Sometimes we got more chiggers picking blackberries than we got blackberries. Chigger bites really hurt and itched like crazy. It was hot work, too; and the briars always scratched me. It wasn't one of my favorite pastimes, and I whined with my usual fervor. We often picked blackberries and sold buckets full—door to door—to the city folks. It was another way to earn some extra money.

One day I had picked a big foot tub plumb full of blackberries and was taking a break, wading in the branch. (I took a whole lot of breaks.) Daddy always said that I was lazy, and I never once argued with him about his astute observation. Well, when I got back to the bucket, one of Uncle Frank's milk cows had her nose down in it and was chomping away at my hard work. When she saw me coming after her with a big stick, she jerked her purple-stained nose out of the bucket and took off. I had to pick more blackberries just to top off the bucket and make everything look really good. Then, Daddy took that cow-slobbered bucket of blackberries to town and sold the whole thing. He was a <u>good</u> daddy! He told the customer the truth about my encounter with the bovine thief and discounted the somewhat mushy bucket of blackberries. I got a whole dollar for my bucketful, but Roger and Laura got two dollars apiece for theirs. Life just wasn't fair.

I have good memories of growing up in the country and doing all the things country boys did—thanks to my parents, siblings, and extended family that had the imagination to make it all entertaining and fun. Memories of camping out and berry picking are among some of my favorite recollections.

# Swimming Holes and Homemade Swings

We went to the Catawba River every day after our chores were done—if we could talk Daddy into taking us. We would drive down to the end of Brawley School Road and turn right on Bethel Church Road. Bethel Church Road became Unity Church Road in Lincoln County as soon as it crossed the river. There was a dirt lane, just past the old Beattie's Ford steel bridge, that led to the left through some woods, and to the river's edge. We would park the car at the river's edge and head for the huge sand bar. It was a favorite spot for swimmers and sunbathers.

**My buddy Dwight Neill at Beattie's Ford Beach**

One day, when I was about five years old, the river was pretty calm, so Daddy took me out into the deep water while riding me on an inner tube. I felt safe. After all, my daddy was with me. He asked me if I would like to learn how to swim. Of course, I said, "Yes," after seeing Roger and Laura splashing around and having a ball. All of a sudden, Daddy pushed me through the hole in that tube and took off down stream with it in his possession. There was nothing else to do but start kicking and paddling. Pretty soon, I had the hang of that swimming stuff. I finally reached him, and he gave me a big hug and helped me back on the tube. Daddy was really excited and told me that I had just learned how to swim. It was that easy, and that concluded my swimming lessons! We all loved the water and swam every time we had the opportunity.

**Steel bridge where we went swimming**

Mama always said that her daddy wouldn't let her go into the water until she learned how to swim. (I never have figured out Papaw's thinking on that one.) She didn't like to

61

go under the water or even get her hair wet. To tell you the truth, I don't know why she even bothered to get in the water at all. She never really learned to swim—but in a pinch she could dog paddle a little bit.

I don't suppose many summers went by that we didn't dam up the branch to make our own swimming hole. We would tote shovels on our shoulders and head for the pasture behind Grandma's house for the building of the great pond. Roger, being the oldest, was usually the chief engineer and always in charge. He would have a spot already picked out for the project, and the work would begin. I watched as he threw the first shovel-full of dirt into the branch and I couldn't tell it made a whole lot of difference. Then he would follow with another, then another. Pretty soon, after watching him do all this work, I would get a little tired and ask him when the pond would be ready for swimming. I suppose I thought that the work should have been progressing a lot faster. He would give me "that look", and I could tell he didn't appreciate the question very much.

Joe and Laura helped, too; but the work was painfully slow. I have to admit, right here, that I wasn't much help. I got better, though, as I got older. Finally, the dam would be four or five feet high, and the water would start backing up. It took a few days for the pond to be deep enough for swimming.

The day finally came when all was ready. Roger, Laura, Joe, and I would christen our magnificent pond with a long run down the pasture hill, culminating with a huge splash. There was one bank that was higher than the other one, and it was used for some serious jumping and diving. The mud from the bottom of the pond was usually stirred up so much that you could pick the water up in your hand and not even see your palm. The color of the water made no difference to us—it was water, it was cool, and it was deep enough for us to swim. That was all we needed.

Uncle Gordon's cows would often wade out in our pond to cool off. I didn't like that very much—you never knew what else they did in that water. Whatever those cows did in the water didn't hurt us, though.

Laura's ears would stay infected all summer, and we just couldn't imagine what was causing it. I think Mama had a pretty good idea though. She kept telling us not to go under that nasty water so much, but we just couldn't have a good time unless we did.

Swimming underwater was half the fun. We did this thing called the "Indian Swim". All it amounted to was holding our hands together over our heads like we were praying, and moving them backward and forward above water while we propelled ourselves under the water by kicking up a storm. It didn't impress a whole lot of folks, but we thought it was really special. I don't ever remember anyone coming down to the pond and lining up, just to witness the "Indian Swim". However, I was proud that I could swim the entire width of the pond underwater while holding my breath. I thought that was pretty cool for a little kid.

There was a rather large hill that ran down to the pond from the pasture. One day, Roger brought the door that came off our old chicken coop and rigged it up to make a ramp. It seemed to be a logical thing for him to do—he was always inventing or building something. We didn't have a ski jump; but by golly, we could have a bicycle jump. We had hoped the elevation of the ramp would propel us out over the water a good ways and possibly all the way to the other side, but it didn't work quite that well. With great bravery, Joe was the first to fly down the hill to attempt the perilous flight. He hit the ramp at a fairly good clip but stalled in midair and crashed into the water, only about six feet from take off. Well, the rest of us had to try and break that pitiful record. The mark was finally surpassed when Roger sailed about ten or twelve feet before his historic, record-breaking splashdown. We never did reach the other side. I really don't think anybody would have believed us if we had.

Nevertheless, I thought Roger's flight was quite impressive. I suppose the record still stands today in the annals of "Swimming Hole Ramp Jumping."

We also built another pond in Uncle Frank's pasture. It was near the big rock where we liked to camp. The stream was a little bigger; too, because it started way up behind Grandma's in the pinewoods. It was a major pond, and the water was way over our heads in places. It was just right for some big-time swimming.

A big snake lived at the end of our pond near a large rock. He would swim down to where we were swimming and check out what was going on. We made so much noise that we usually kept him scared off and out of our territory. We got along really well with that snake. He never bothered us at all; but it was always fun to see the reactions from the first-time visitors that went swimming with us.

It has been at least forty-five or fifty years since we had our swimming hole in Uncle Frank's pasture and that old snake's home is probably gone by now. The Winbourne Housing Development on Rinehardt Road encompasses the property where the pond was located and I can't even find the big rock anymore.

Uncle Frank's property was like a special piece of Heaven that had wonderful pastures and streams and woods and kudzu gullies. Uncle Frank was Grandpa Joe Ketchie's brother and our great uncle. I couldn't imagine us calling him Great Uncle Frank every time we talked about him. He was a great uncle though, and had a lot of places for a boy to get into trouble and have fun.

One time, Roger climbed a huge tree that leaned out over his kudzu gully and rigged up a piece of strong cable on an outstretched limb. The cable was then fitted with a crosspiece so we could get a good grip and hold on to it for dear life as we swung out over the deep gully.

My turn had arrived to swing, and I was determined that I would not be out done. I was not a very big boy. In fact, I was so skinny that, if I drank a Cheerwine and walked out into the sun, I looked like a thermometer. Nevertheless, I got a good, running start and flew off the bank of that gully hollering like Tarzan. My plan was to swing all the way around that leaning tree and land back on the same bank from where I had just taken off. I had seen it done before by the older boys and it didn't look like such a big deal to me.

Well, in mid-swing I got turned around backwards and hit that tree with a big <u>WHUMP</u> with the back of my head and the rest of my scrawny, little body. When I hit the ground, all the breath left me in an instant; and I saw stars, moons, planets, and about half the solar system before my eyes finally uncrossed. I did, however, land on my back and not on my head. I had just used my head to attack that tree, and it couldn't stand a whole lot more damage. I could hear someone up on the bank yelling at Roger, "Your mama's goin' to kill you." Well, Roger couldn't help that his crazy, little brother was dumb enough to try that dangerous trip around the tree. I never told anyone that I was going to attempt it—it was kind of a spur of the moment thing. Roger always felt he was responsible for me and took my safety seriously. They all rushed down the bank, tripping over the kudzu, and ended up sprawled at the bottom of the gully, in a pile, alongside me. Roger consoled me while we waited for my breathing to return to normal, and it finally did. I was all right in an hour or so and started swinging again, but I didn't take that dangerous route anymore. I wasn't <u>that</u> stupid; I left that one for the big boys. Mama didn't have to kill Roger, either, because she never found out about my "brush with death".

One day, Roger built a tall platform and we installed it on the bank of the gully. This added height would enable us to climb higher, for a stronger take-off. The extra speed generated by the height would help us to go farther.

Charles Nantz wanted to be the first one to give it a try. We helped him ascend the platform and extended the cable up to him. I still remember that day; it was a warm, Sunday afternoon; Charles had gone to church, and was proudly wearing his new, dressy, wine-colored pants. All eyes were on him as he readied himself to make the valiant leap. All of a sudden, he gave a loud yell and leaped off that platform with all the hopes of landing completely on the other side of the gully. That feat had never yet been accomplished and that was the reason for the added height of the platform.

It was not the best time for the cable to break. Just as Charles was starting his downward thrust, the cable snapped. Poor Charles hit the ground with his rear end and slid all the way down to the bottom of the gully, ripping the entire seat out of his wine-colored britches. We all laughed and laughed as Charles made his way back up the gully bank. He was almost crying because he had ruined his favorite Sunday pants. I don't think the cable was ever fastened to that tree again. It would have been too hard to top what Charles Nantz did on the maiden voyage.

**Charles Nantz 1958**

Not very long after that momentous occasion, Charles was killed in a tragic motorcycle accident less than a half-mile from our house. It happened just a few days after he graduated from Mooresville Senior High School in 1958. We still miss him.

# Rabbit and Squirrel Hunting

We always looked forward to Thanksgiving Day with great anticipation. Rabbit hunting season opened with a loud bang all over the surrounding area near where we lived north of Mooresville. You could hear shotguns going off throughout the countryside, from Mazeppa to Shepherds. It sounded like a young war had been declared.

There were four Black and Tan hounds that were kept down at Daddy's older sister, Aunt Sarah Belk's, house. Drum, Queen, Bell, and Bud were their names and those dogs lived to hunt. They were great, multi-talented hunting dogs. It's a good thing they weren't union because we used them for "possum hunting", too; and we never gave them time off for vacation or sick days either.

Aunt Sarah's two boys, Pete and David, Uncle Gordon, Joe, Daddy, Roger, David Wilson, and I would gather at Aunt Sarah's house for coffee early on Thanksgiving morning and get ready for the big hunt. (It was a tradition.) We would start behind Aunt Sarah's house and see what we could jump. It usually didn't take too long to get a good race going. Daddy always said that hearing the dogs run while chasing a rabbit was music to his ears. I didn't know about the music part, but I sure liked to eat those rabbits.

We would go all the way up to the woods behind Uncle Frank Ketchie's house, down to the pasture behind Grandma's, back below Aunt Sarah's around the old Blackwelder place, and then all the way to the creek below Uncle Tom Brantley's over on Highway 21. Those dogs would chase rabbits all over the place. Sometimes the rabbits would get into a brush pile and that would drive the dogs

## Cowboys and Indians

I played Cowboys and Indians with just about anyone that would play with me. I had a genuine Stallion .45 cap pistol. It even had bullets that you could take apart, place the caps inside of them, and reload them in the cylinder—just like a real gun. It had plastic handles that looked just like real pearl. It was just too cool! I got killed a lot in my cowboy days, but I killed my share of bad guys, too.

**My Stallion 45 cap pistol**

Donnie Lambert lived just two doors down the road, and we played Cowboys a lot. Most of the time, we left the Indians alone. I think he had a two-gun rig, but I was faster on the draw. I was a little older than he was, and I didn't let him kill me as often as he would have liked. Being the oldest, for a change, was definitely an advantage. We made hideouts behind the calf stable and would play some serious Cowboys in the woods where you could hide behind the trees and underbrush. We really liked going down to Uncle Frank's pasture where there were a lot of big rocks. We

crazy because they couldn't get to them. We would have to start taking the brush off the pile by hand until we got close enough to the rabbits to force them to make a run for it.

All the older guys carried shotguns but I never liked them. (They made way too much noise for me.) I carried my little .22 caliber Springfield rifle. One of the highlights of my childhood hunting trips was shooting a rabbit with my rifle after everybody else had already missed him with their shotguns.

Pete and David Belk got married and left home; and just about everyone else had quit hunting except Roger and David Wilson. Those two boys would faithfully go down to Aunt Sarah's after school to take the old hounds hunting. All four dogs would be sitting out at the end of the driveway looking for Roger's car everyday. When they saw it rounding the curve that led to Aunt Sarah's house, they would start barking like crazy. They couldn't wait to go chase some unfortunate critter "seven ways from Sunday".

All of Aunt Sarah's hounds eventually passed away and went to the big "rabbit hunt in the sky"; so Daddy and Roger bought themselves some beagles so they wouldn't have to give up hunting. Those little beagles could really run a rabbit. Daddy named his dog, "Whitey", and the other dogs belonged to Roger.

That doggoned beagle of Daddy's would never stay in the lot even though there was an eight-foot fence around the entire enclosure. It used to really upset Daddy because he couldn't figure out how "Whitey" kept escaping his confines. One day, he decided to watch until he found out how that dog was getting out of his very secure surroundings.

Daddy had built a sturdy lot with angled braces that ran from the ground all the way to the top of the corner posts. The eight-foot fence was solidly fastened to the ground all the way around the perimeter of the lot. It was thought to have been escape proof. That was not the case with old "Whitey". That smart beagle would wedge himself between

the angled brace and the wire of the fence, and then push with his back while he inched his way up the brace. He would do this until he reached the top of the fence and politely jump down on the other side, to freedom. He was an amazing dog and he really didn't like to be penned up.

Roger, David, and Daddy hunted with those little beagle dogs regularly. By this time, I had retired from my rabbit hunting trips—I had discovered girls. After that fantastic revelation, I never missed hunting at all!

**Daddy with "Whitey" and Roger's beagles**

However, I did go squirrel hunting just about every after school in the wintertime. Most days, I would across the Statesville Highway and quietly tiptoe into Lil' Patten's woods. Aunt Lil' Patten was Grandpa Ketchie's sister and lived across the road from Grandm house with her daughter Lillian. There, I would find a go warm place to sit against an old oak tree, and just wait some unsuspecting squirrel to come close enough for me get a decent shot at him.

I loved going to those woods and looked forward to th quiet time I could spend alone while waiting for som squirrels to make their appearance. It was also a place could go and smoke a cigarette—supposedly without anyone knowing. Mama would ask me as soon as I came through the back door, "Have you been smoking?" I had my usual response ready, "Me, smoking?" Heck, I didn't know she could smell the smoke on my clothes. I never did smoke in front of my parents and I eventually gave up that nasty smoking habit in 1968.

I brought home quite a few squirrels for the supper table in my hunting days. Roger usually had to clean them, though. I always acted dumb; like I didn't know how to clean the things. I could do the job once in a while, but could never do it as fast as Roger. I was never able to do it with the same fervor that he mustered for the task, either. In fact, I hated the job and that was reason enough for letting Roger be in charge of "wild animal cleaning".

I liked hunting squirrels better than hunting rabbits—I got to sit down while I was hunting squirrels. Rabbit hunting was a very tiring sport.

The hunting trips were always enjoyed by everyone and provided meat for the tables of the hungry Ketchie clan.

could jump off of those rocks onto the backs of the bad guys when they came by unsuspectingly. However, neither one of us was very good at back jumping—not many bad guys came by so we could practice our craft.

One summer, Roger made some homemade arrows, using the points from a few darts that he found. He fastened them to the tips of reeds that he harvested from the creek bank. (Roger was already into recycling.) The arrows didn't look so hot without any feathers; so he tried to fasten some to them. He couldn't get them to stay on very well; so he just shot the arrows without the feathers.

Roger and I were playing Cowboys and Indians one day and we decided to use real ammunition. I was hiding from him behind the calf stable and saw him as he popped his head around the corner. I didn't have time to think. I just fired off a shot at him with my Red Ryder BB Gun. It hit him almost between the eyes—maybe just a little bit higher. It made a real pretty mark that was starting to turn bright red. Being shot by his little brother made Roger a very disgruntled young man! He retaliated by shooting me with his homemade bow and arrow as I was running past him. The arrow hit my leg with a thump. I had on short pants and could plainly see that arrow sticking all the way in my leg, up to where the dart point was fastened to the shaft. It looked so funny that I started laughing, but then the pain hit me. The laughing was short lived. I started squalling "bloody murder" and headed for the house.

Mama came out of the back door when she heard the commotion. She took one look at the arrow sticking out of my leg and promptly took poor Roger's longbow from him and just broke it in half—right before his eyes. The next and obvious thing to do was remove the arrow. It didn't have a barb or anything; so Roger just jerked it out—pretty as you please. The way Mama was acting, you would have thought he was practicing medicine without a license. Once he took the arrow out of my leg, I felt much better. Roger and I had pretty much made up by this time, but Mama was the one who was still having problems with the whole situation.

I really believe the arrow incident was the defining moment that Mama decided to go to work in the cotton mill.

"The arrow," Roger, Laura, and me

Daddy took over the raising of the unpredictable issues of his marriage. He was a patient man—up to a point. We would just have to learn where that point was. Roger made another longbow or two for himself, and I played with the BB gun running on empty. Our lives were never the same after that. Daddy always seemed to find something for us to do that required our energies to be focused toward a common good—like working in the garden.

I remember how difficult it was for me to cock that BB gun. I would have to place the stock against my right foot, lean the barrel over toward my left leg, and pull up on the lever as hard as I could with my right hand. Sometimes I still couldn't cock it. I was what you would call, a "weakling". Since Roger was a lot bigger than I was, he had no problem cocking the thing. I asked him to do it for me an awful lot.

One day, Roger came up with another of his brilliant ideas. (His ideas always seemed to affect me adversely!) We went into Uncle Frank's woods, and Roger promptly took his station on the stump of an old hickory tree. My role was to hide behind a tree until I was called upon to do as I was instructed. He sat on the stump with my BB gun (not cocked) standing upright between his legs. All I had to do was run from one tree to another. It sounded pretty simple to me, but it didn't take long before I realized what he was going to do. When I started to make my run, he picked up the BB gun, cocked it, and shot me before I got to the next tree. The saddest thing about the whole affair is that he hit me just about every, single, solitary time. He was a gentleman, though, and just shot me below the waist. Roger knew what it was like to get hit between the eyes; so he was a merciful big brother.

Hal Blackwelder and his sister, Patsy, lived next door to us and were the offspring of Mr. June and Mrs. Essie Blackwelder. Patsy used to change my diapers and hold me on her lap. I don't remember much about that, but she swears that it's true, and she would never lie to me. Hal didn't play with us rough Ketchie kids too often. We were occasionally known to have bounced some of those great big, green, chestnut acorns off his head—by accident, of course. We mostly shot them with our slingshots. Good ammunition was hard to come by.

Hal was a quiet, studious boy who loved to draw. I would go to his house often just to watch him use his pencil to make fashion models appear on his sketchpad. He was truly amazing. If I could have drawn women like he did, I would have probably stayed inside the house and drawn my life away.

One bright, summer day, Hal joined us in a hotly contested game of Cowboys. We were playing at Grandma's house where there were a lot of places to hide. Hal had been captured and incarcerated in our jail. The jail was an abandoned, outdoor shower that was attached to the back wall of the smokehouse. Uncle Gordon, had at one time, installed a fifty-five-gallon barrel on some crossbeams overhead, then fitted some curtains around the outside of the structure. All you had to do to take a shower was to fill up the barrel in the morning and let the sun warm the water for you during the day. Then, you just walked in, closed the curtain, and pulled the rope that released the water in the barrel; and presto, there was your shower. It was crude, but it worked for them. They never used this shower after the bathroom was built inside the house; so the old shower had become our jail. The curtains were gone and the bare wall of the smokehouse was exposed to the sun and that is where Uncle Gordon dried his red-hot chili peppers. We locked Hal in there by himself. Nobody had ever escaped from our jail, and we were proud of its security.

Knowing Hal, we were pretty sure that he would stay where we put him. We had chosen sides and had not captured anybody except Hal; he was our only prisoner. We definitely couldn't afford to lose him. Things were going pretty well until we heard this awful screaming coming from behind the smokehouse. Then, there was a terrible, crashing sound, followed by more hollering. Here came Hal, rounding the corner of the smokehouse like a flash of lightning and heading straight for the rain barrel. Hal stuck his head under the water and came up for air just like he had been baptized. I could see tears in his eyes, but he hadn't been crying. He came as close to cussin' as I had ever seen him.

However, I did go squirrel hunting just [...] after school in the wintertime. Most da[...] across the Statesville Highway and qui[...] Lil' Patten's woods. Aunt Lil' Pa[...] Ketchie's sister and lived across [...] house with her daughter Lillian [...] warm place to sit against an [...] some unsuspecting squirrel [...] get a decent shot at him.

I loved going to th[...] quiet time I could [...] squirrels to make [...] could go and sm[...] knowing. Ma[...] back door, [...] response ready, [...] could smell the sm[...] front of my parents [...] smoking habit in 1968.

I brought home quite a fe[...] in my hunting days. Roger us[...] though. I always acted dumb; like [...] clean the things. I could do the job once [...] never do it as fast as Roger. I was never abl[...] same fervor that he mustered for the task, ei[...] hated the job and that was reason enough for letting [...] in charge of "wild animal cleaning".

I liked hunting squirrels better than hunting rabbits [...] got to sit down while I was hunting squirrels. Rabbit hunting [...] was a very tiring sport.

The hunting trips were always enjoyed by everyone and provided meat for the tables of the hungry Ketchie clan.

crazy because they couldn't get to them. We would ha[ve...] start taking the brush off the pile by hand until we got [...] enough to the rabbits to force them to make a run for it.

All the older guys carried shotguns but I never [...] them. (They made way too much noise for me.) I carried [...] little .22 caliber Springfield rifle. One of the highlights of [...] childhood hunting trips was shooting a rabbit with my ri[fle...] after everybody else had already missed him with the[ir...] shotguns.

Pete and David Belk got married and left home; and just about everyone else had quit hunting except Roger and David Wilson. Those two boys would faithfully go down to Aunt Sarah's after school to take the old hounds hunting. All four dogs would be sitting out at the end of the driveway looking for Roger's car everyday. When they saw it rounding the curve that led to Aunt Sarah's house, they would start barking like crazy. They couldn't wait to go chase some unfortunate critter "seven ways from Sunday".

All of Aunt Sarah's hounds eventually passed away and went to the big "rabbit hunt in the sky"; so Daddy and Roger bought themselves some beagles so they wouldn't have to give up hunting. Those little beagles could really run a rabbit. Daddy named his dog, "Whitey", and the other dogs belonged to Roger.

That doggoned beagle of Daddy's would never stay in the lot even though there was an eight-foot fence around the entire enclosure. It used to really upset Daddy because he couldn't figure out how "Whitey" kept escaping his confines.

One day, he decided to watch until he found out how that dog was getting out of his very secure surroundings.

Daddy had built a sturdy lot with angled braces that ran from the ground all the way to the top of the corner posts. The eight-foot fence was solidly fastened to the ground all the way around the perimeter of the lot. It was thought to have been escape proof. That was not the case with old "Whitey". That smart beagle would wedge himself between

Daddy with "Whitey" and Roger's beagles

# Cowboys and Indians

I played Cowboys and Indians with just about anyone that would play with me. I had a genuine Stallion .45 cap pistol. It even had bullets that you could take apart, place the caps inside of them, and reload them in the cylinder—just like a real gun. It had plastic handles that looked just like real pearl. It was just too cool! I got killed a lot in my cowboy days, but I killed my share of bad guys, too.

**My Stallion 45 cap pistol**

Donnie Lambert lived just two doors down the road, and we played Cowboys a lot. Most of the time, we left the Indians alone. I think he had a two-gun rig, but I was faster on the draw. I was a little older than he was, and I didn't let him kill me as often as he would have liked. Being the oldest, for a change, was definitely an advantage. We made hideouts behind the calf stable and would play some serious Cowboys in the woods where you could hide behind the trees and underbrush. We really liked going down to Uncle Frank's pasture where there were a lot of big rocks. We

could jump off of those rocks onto the backs of the bad guys when they came by unsuspectingly. However, neither one of us was very good at back jumping—not many bad guys came by so we could practice our craft.

One summer, Roger made some homemade arrows, using the points from a few darts that he found. He fastened them to the tips of reeds that he harvested from the creek bank. (Roger was already into recycling.) The arrows didn't look so hot without any feathers; so he tried to fasten some to them. He couldn't get them to stay on very well; so he just shot the arrows without the feathers.

Roger and I were playing Cowboys and Indians one day and we decided to use real ammunition. I was hiding from him behind the calf stable and saw him as he popped his head around the corner. I didn't have time to think. I just fired off a shot at him with my Red Ryder BB Gun. It hit him almost between the eyes—maybe just a little bit higher. It made a real pretty mark that was starting to turn bright red. Being shot by his little brother made Roger a very disgruntled young man! He retaliated by shooting me with his homemade bow and arrow as I was running past him. The arrow hit my leg with a thump. I had on short pants and could plainly see that arrow sticking all the way in my leg, up to where the dart point was fastened to the shaft. It looked so funny that I started laughing, but then the pain hit me. The laughing was short lived. I started squalling "bloody murder" and headed for the house.

Mama came out of the back door when she heard the commotion. She took one look at the arrow sticking out of my leg and promptly took poor Roger's longbow from him and just broke it in half—right before his eyes. The next and obvious thing to do was remove the arrow. It didn't have a barb or anything; so Roger just jerked it out—pretty as you please. The way Mama was acting, you would have thought he was practicing medicine without a license. Once he took the arrow out of my leg, I felt much better. Roger and I had

pretty much made up by this time, but Mama was the one who was still having problems with the whole situation.

I really believe the arrow incident was the defining moment that Mama decided to go to work in the cotton mill.

**"The arrow," Roger, Laura, and me**

Daddy took over the raising of the unpredictable issues of his marriage. He was a patient man—up to a point. We would just have to learn where that point was. Roger made another longbow or two for himself, and I played with the BB gun running on empty. Our lives were never the same after that. Daddy always seemed to find something for us to

do that required our energies to be focused toward a common good—like working in the garden.

I remember how difficult it was for me to cock that BB gun. I would have to place the stock against my right foot, lean the barrel over toward my left leg, and pull up on the lever as hard as I could with my right hand. Sometimes I still couldn't cock it. I was what you would call, a "weakling". Since Roger was a lot bigger than I was, he had no problem cocking the thing. I asked him to do it for me an awful lot.

One day, Roger came up with another of his brilliant ideas. (His ideas always seemed to affect me adversely!) We went into Uncle Frank's woods, and Roger promptly took his station on the stump of an old hickory tree. My role was to hide behind a tree until I was called upon to do as I was instructed. He sat on the stump with my BB gun (not cocked) standing upright between his legs. All I had to do was run from one tree to another. It sounded pretty simple to me, but it didn't take long before I realized what he was going to do. When I started to make my run, he picked up the BB gun, cocked it, and shot me before I got to the next tree. The saddest thing about the whole affair is that he hit me just about every, single, solitary time. He was a gentleman, though, and just shot me below the waist. Roger knew what it was like to get hit between the eyes; so he was a merciful big brother.

Hal Blackwelder and his sister, Patsy, lived next door to us and were the offspring of Mr. June and Mrs. Essie Blackwelder. Patsy used to change my diapers and hold me on her lap. I don't remember much about that, but she swears that it's true, and she would never lie to me. Hal didn't play with us rough Ketchie kids too often. We were occasionally known to have bounced some of those great big, green, chestnut acorns off his head—by accident, of course. We mostly shot them with our slingshots. Good ammunition was hard to come by.

Hal was a quiet, studious boy who loved to draw. I would go to his house often just to watch him use his pencil to make fashion models appear on his sketchpad. He was truly amazing. If I could have drawn women like he did, I would have probably stayed inside the house and drawn my life away.

One bright, summer day, Hal joined us in a hotly contested game of Cowboys. We were playing at Grandma's house where there were a lot of places to hide. Hal had been captured and incarcerated in our jail. The jail was an abandoned, outdoor shower that was attached to the back wall of the smokehouse. Uncle Gordon, had at one time, installed a fifty-five-gallon barrel on some crossbeams overhead, then fitted some curtains around the outside of the structure. All you had to do to take a shower was to fill up the barrel in the morning and let the sun warm the water for you during the day. Then, you just walked in, closed the curtain, and pulled the rope that released the water in the barrel; and presto, there was your shower. It was crude, but it worked for them. They never used this shower after the bathroom was built inside the house; so the old shower had become our jail. The curtains were gone and the bare wall of the smokehouse was exposed to the sun and that is where Uncle Gordon dried his red-hot chili peppers. We locked Hal in there by himself. Nobody had ever escaped from our jail, and we were proud of its security.

Knowing Hal, we were pretty sure that he would stay where we put him. We had chosen sides and had not captured anybody except Hal; he was our only prisoner. We definitely couldn't afford to lose him. Things were going pretty well until we heard this awful screaming coming from behind the smokehouse. Then, there was a terrible, crashing sound, followed by more hollering. Here came Hal, rounding the corner of the smokehouse like a flash of lightning and heading straight for the rain barrel. Hal stuck his head under the water and came up for air just like he had been baptized. I could see tears in his eyes, but he hadn't been crying. He came as close to cussin' as I had ever seen him.

crazy because they couldn't get to them. We would have to start taking the brush off the pile by hand until we got close enough to the rabbits to force them to make a run for it.

All the older guys carried shotguns but I never liked them. (They made way too much noise for me.) I carried my little .22 caliber Springfield rifle. One of the highlights of my childhood hunting trips was shooting a rabbit with my rifle after everybody else had already missed him with their shotguns.

Pete and David Belk got married and left home; and just about everyone else had quit hunting except Roger and David Wilson. Those two boys would faithfully go down to Aunt Sarah's after school to take the old hounds hunting. All four dogs would be sitting out at the end of the driveway looking for Roger's car everyday. When they saw it rounding the curve that led to Aunt Sarah's house, they would start barking like crazy. They couldn't wait to go chase some unfortunate critter "seven ways from Sunday".

All of Aunt Sarah's hounds eventually passed away and went to the big "rabbit hunt in the sky"; so Daddy and Roger bought themselves some beagles so they wouldn't have to give up hunting. Those little beagles could really run a rabbit. Daddy named his dog, "Whitey", and the other dogs belonged to Roger.

That doggoned beagle of Daddy's would never stay in the lot even though there was an eight-foot fence around the entire enclosure. It used to really upset Daddy because he couldn't figure out how "Whitey" kept escaping his confines. One day, he decided to watch until he found out how that dog was getting out of his very secure surroundings.

Daddy had built a sturdy lot with angled braces that ran from the ground all the way to the top of the corner posts. The eight-foot fence was solidly fastened to the ground all the way around the perimeter of the lot. It was thought to have been escape proof. That was not the case with old "Whitey". That smart beagle would wedge himself between

the angled brace and the wire of the fence, and then push with his back while he inched his way up the brace. He would do this until he reached the top of the fence and politely jump down on the other side, to freedom. He was an amazing dog and he really didn't like to be penned up.

Roger, David, and Daddy hunted with those little beagle dogs regularly. By this time, I had retired from my rabbit hunting trips—I had discovered girls. After that fantastic revelation, I never missed hunting at all!

**Daddy with "Whitey" and Roger's beagles**

However, I did go squirrel hunting just about everyday after school in the wintertime. Most days, I would walk across the Statesville Highway and quietly tiptoe into Aunt Lil' Patten's woods. Aunt Lil' Patten was Grandpa Joe Ketchie's sister and lived across the road from Grandma's house with her daughter Lillian. There, I would find a good warm place to sit against an old oak tree, and just wait for some unsuspecting squirrel to come close enough for me to get a decent shot at him.

I loved going to those woods and looked forward to the quiet time I could spend alone while waiting for some squirrels to make their appearance. It was also a place I could go and smoke a cigarette—supposedly without anyone knowing. Mama would ask me as soon as I came through the back door, "Have you been smoking?" I had my usual response ready, "Me, smoking?" Heck, I didn't know she could smell the smoke on my clothes. I never did smoke in front of my parents and I eventually gave up that nasty smoking habit in 1968.

I brought home quite a few squirrels for the supper table in my hunting days. Roger usually had to clean them, though. I always acted dumb; like I didn't know how to clean the things. I could do the job once in a while, but could never do it as fast as Roger. I was never able to do it with the same fervor that he mustered for the task, either. In fact, I hated the job and that was reason enough for letting Roger be in charge of "wild animal cleaning".

I liked hunting squirrels better than hunting rabbits—I got to sit down while I was hunting squirrels. Rabbit hunting was a very tiring sport.

The hunting trips were always enjoyed by everyone and provided meat for the tables of the hungry Ketchie clan.

# Cowboys and Indians

I played Cowboys and Indians with just about anyone that would play with me. I had a genuine Stallion .45 cap pistol. It even had bullets that you could take apart, place the caps inside of them, and reload them in the cylinder—just like a real gun. It had plastic handles that looked just like real pearl. It was just too cool! I got killed a lot in my cowboy days, but I killed my share of bad guys, too.

**My Stallion 45 cap pistol**

Donnie Lambert lived just two doors down the road, and we played Cowboys a lot. Most of the time, we left the Indians alone. I think he had a two-gun rig, but I was faster on the draw. I was a little older than he was, and I didn't let him kill me as often as he would have liked. Being the oldest, for a change, was definitely an advantage. We made hideouts behind the calf stable and would play some serious Cowboys in the woods where you could hide behind the trees and underbrush. We really liked going down to Uncle Frank's pasture where there were a lot of big rocks. We

**Our jail was attached behind the smokehouse**

While being imprisoned, Hal had gotten bored and decided to munch on some of Uncle Gordon's colorful, red peppers. That boy tore our holding cell into such disrepair that we couldn't use it anymore. Hal went down in history as the only desperado to escape from the Ketchie boys' jail.

Some of the greatest memories that I can conjure up were related to my childhood play. Hal was an inspiration to me and perhaps was one of the reasons I decided to become an artist. Hal passed away a few years ago, and I miss his enthusiasm for art. I am the proud owner of an oil painting he did of his mother.

I still have that cap pistol.

# Bows and Arrows and Spears and Things

My brother, Roger, was quite an inventor. He was always working in our shop, dreaming up something really neat—usually to try out on me.

One day, he asked me to go to Grandma's house and stand in the front yard. "When you get there, just stand still and don't move," he said.

Naturally, I agreed and said, "OK", being five years younger and the trusting sort that I was. I ran down there as fast as my little, nine-year-old legs could carry me, kicking up a dust trail on Grandma's driveway with my bare feet.

Roger had aged a piece of ash wood for about a year in the ceiling of Daddy's woodworking shop and had finally made a longbow just like Robin Hood had used. That's what he told me, anyway. I believed just about anything he told me.

I didn't have to stand there too long before I discovered what he had in mind. He notched one of his arrows in that longbow, stretched it way out, and let it fly. I watched that arrow as it climbed a long way up in the sky; then suddenly, it started coming down in a graceful arch. I wasn't real smart, but I could see that it was coming down straight at me with surprising speed. I didn't ask Roger for permission to move; I took off running for the safety of Grandma's porch. That arrow made a horrible sound as it kathunked into the ground where I was standing a moment before. I do believe it was one of his better shots. (That was a very long distance.) He yelled down to me, "Since you're already there, bring back my arrow."

Roger did the same thing while frog gigging. He, David Wilson, and I were gigging frogs one summer night when they sighted a great big frog across the water, at the end of Dr. Sholar's pond. Well, you might guess what my job was to be. They held the lights on the frog, and I was instructed to go all the way around the pond and get close enough to gig him. After much difficulty traversing around the backwater, I found him still sitting there as pretty as could be. As I brought the gig back to lunge it into that huge frog, an arrow flew all the way from across the water and stuck that thing to the ground before I could move. I waited for the usual appeal from Roger, "Since you're already there, bring back my arrow. Bring the frog, too."

Well, I started around the pond, concentrating on carrying the frog and that doggoned arrow, and carelessly stepped into some quicksand. When I started sinking down into that stuff really fast, I became frightened. (That's like being scared to death.) I started yelling for Roger to help me, but I suppose he thought I was just in one of my whining modes. They yelled for me to pull hard on one foot while I pushed down with the other one. When I tried to pull one foot out, the other one would go down even deeper. I eventually sank almost up to my waist and still didn't feel any solid ground. By this time, I was getting really scared, and I think that they were getting a little concerned, too. David and Roger finally made their way around to where I was stuck and carefully extended a limb to me. I grabbed hold of it and they finally freed me from my dangerous predicament, but I was covered with slime and wet quicksand over half my body.

The worst thing about the whole situation was being made to ride in the trunk of David's car on the way home because my clothes and I were in such an awful mess. Being the fine, upstanding, young men that they were, they took me to David's house where they washed me off with a garden hose in the back yard—clothes and all.

One year, Daddy rigged up an old telephone pole cross-arm between two oak trees in the backyard and fixed it up for a swing. Roger made a trapeze for himself out of some chain and an old piece of water pipe, and he practiced on that thing everyday. He could swing upside down by his legs and slide all the way down—inch by inch—until he would be swinging by just his heels. I guess he saw them do that on *Super Circus* while watching Aunt Ruth's television. That feat never ceased to amaze me. I couldn't get over the thought of having a brother that could do something that impressive. I had trouble just holding on with both my hands. I was not very coordinated.

We tired of that swinging stuff after a few weeks and were looking for bigger and better things to do with our time. If we didn't stay busy, Daddy would have us pulling up grass in the garden or find something else for us to do to keep us out of trouble.

Roger, being in one of his inventive moods, rigged an old, bicycle, inner-tube between the two-swing hangers, and then looped it over the cross-arm to make a terrific slingshot of gigantic proportions. I couldn't wait to see what was going to happen next. I believe he had been thinking about this for some time because he brought out a huge spear-looking thing that he made out of a sapling. It was about six or seven feet long. I got all excited when he put that sucker up on the cross-arm and backed it into the inner tube. He pulled and pulled until the very end of the spear barely extended over the cross-arm. When he let go, it made a loud swishing sound, and you could hear that inner tube flapping in the wind. That spear took off and sailed majestically through the air, all the way across our back yard, and promptly slammed into the side of Mr. Malcolm's garage. Well, that made Roger about to bust—he was so proud. That was a flight of over seventy-five yards!

It then became evident that it was time to establish a new, spear-shooting record. Roger requested that I run down to Mr. Malcolm's yard and recover the spear before anyone saw what he had done. I ran and got the spear without being seen and brought it back and gave it to Roger. He then reloaded and pulled and pulled the tube again and let her fly. That spear looked like it was going to go all the way over Mr. Malcolm's garage this time, but Roger evidently miscalculated a little bit. It went crashing down onto his tin roof and bounced off all the way over to the other side of the building. We waited a little while to see if any one was going to come out of Mr. Malcolm's house and yell at us. Nobody did, so Roger thought that it might be safe for me to do the spear-retrieval routine again. I returned with the spear in hand to the launching site, but we decided to refrain from shooting spears for a week or two. We thought it wise to wait and see if there were any repercussions from the last, record-breaking shot. Believing there were none; after a couple of weeks, we resumed our spear-shooting salvos for a while longer. Daddy never mentioned our assault on Mr. Malcolm's garage, but before long, found something for us to do that was more suited for the common good of our community. I really think that word had gotten out.

One moonless night after an unsuccessful possum hunt, we gathered in the back yard, horsing around as usual. By this time, the dew had formed all over the grass, and the crisp, fall air was invigorating. We had an electric wire that ran around our hog lot and kept the hogs from rooting under the regular fence by giving them a good jolt of electricity.

Everything was perfect, and the timing was just right for some stupid stuff to happen as boys gather around and look for something to do. Out of the blue, somebody said, "Why don't we see who can hold on to that electric fence the longest?" Well, we all approached this daunting dare with great apprehension, but agreed to grab hold of it at the same time. When all the yelling had stopped, David Wilson was the only one left standing there, holding on to the wire with a huge grin on his face, while he shook all over.

It didn't take long to tire of this dangerous sport when Roger was struck with another one of his brilliant ideas. He dared us to stand still in the dark while he shot one of his lethal, hunting arrows straight up into the air. The plan was to see who had the nerve to be the last one to move. Roger drew back his bow and shot it as straight up as he possibly could, and we all stood there, like a bunch of idiots, looking skyward into the pitch-black night. Suddenly, we heard a swishing sound very rapidly approaching, and we all dove for cover under a picnic table that Daddy had just finished making. That arrow came down with such force into the top of that table that we had to cut it out of the wood with a pocketknife. It centered the table right over our thick skulls. Nobody won, and everyone went home after that. I think the uncertainty of what might have happened next was just too much for them.

When Roger was left alone, he could come up with some interesting inventions. He perfected what he called his "Cannon" one spring day, and we couldn't wait to try it out. The Cannon consisted of a piece of water-pipe with an elbow screwed on to one end. It had a hole drilled through the pipe, near the elbow, where the fuse of a firecracker came out. That was where it got to be a little bit too technical for me. This was his hand-held model.

Roger would take a good-sized firecracker, insert it into the pipe, and pull the fuse up through the hole where it could be lit. Then, when the elbow was tightened securely; the cannon was ready to fire. Roger would then take a big, green acorn from one of our chestnut oaks and place it into the end of the barrel for ammunition. When he lit the fuse, I would always cover my ears. I hated loud noises, but I wouldn't have missed seeing this for anything. He would point that loaded, hand-held cannon at a tin can we had set up as a target and knock the living daylights out of it. Sometimes he would take a short cut and just stick a firecracker under a tin can and light the fuse. It would make a pretty good racket as it sent the can flying through the air.

Roger never had a firearms manufacturing license; but it never deterred him from making weapons of minimal destruction. He forged ahead and made, what we called, his "Super-Deluxe Cannon. The barrel was housed in a wooden contraption with wheels. The deluxe model would back up about three or four inches when fired. He would set that one up when he wanted to make a big impression. I'd line up some of my little toy soldiers for him, and he would mow them down with his cannon. It impressed the heck out of me!

Roger was really adept at inventing things to entertain us. Some of the inventions seemed to invite a bit of trouble, but most of them were a great deal of fun. God blessed and watched over us through these uncertain ventures into the world of sophisticated technology.

# Mischief at Grandma's

I know it's hard to believe, but I was not the perfect child. I tried; Lord, how I tried! It was just not in me. I was curious, mischievous, and sometimes a downright pest. I might have been even a little bit lazy. There you have it; I finally admitted my faults after all these years. I think they have always been common knowledge anyway.

I particularly remember one prime example when Laura and I were really young and were playing make-believe at Grandma's house. Before we left home, we had mixed some cocoa and sugar together, put the mixture in some empty snuff cans, and brought them with us. We were pretending we were dipping snuff. It looked like snuff, too; and it tasted really good. It wouldn't give you cancer, either; but we were warned that it would rot our teeth out. We did it anyway!

Well, this particular day, the ladies from the First Presbyterian Church of Mooresville came to visit Grandma (she was almost a charter member). We thought that was awfully nice of them to pay our poor Grandma a visit. When the ladies of the church were getting out of their big, black Buick, Laura and I pulled our lips way out, turned up the snuff cans, and unceremoniously poured some make-believe snuff into our mouths. I thought those ladies were going to lose it right there, but they composed themselves pretty well. However, they did keep giving us the evil eye. In due course, they warily went into the house and visited with Grandma..

When they were taking their leave and talking with Grandma on the side porch, we made sure they were looking our way before we reloaded our lips one more time. I don't think that went over too well with anybody; but doggone, that was fun.

Cousin Joe and I always seemed to get into some kind of trouble when we were together. I remember one day, being at Grandma's with my Daisy Red Ryder BB Gun and I was shooting anything that moved. I let Joe take a few shots with my new gun, but we were quickly running out of targets. All the birds had already warned each other about me, and my new gun, and had left the area.

Joe set some cans up on the trailer, beneath the barn window for target practice. We were just going to do that a while until something better came along. We were shooting at the cans when one of my shots went astray and hit the corner of the window to the feed room. The BB made a pretty circle in the window glass and Joe said, "Would you look at that?" The circle looked so forlorn there by itself; I just thought it would look a little better if it had one beside it. I didn't place the next shot exactly where I wanted it to go; so I had to shoot again. One thing led to another, and before long the window was decorated with circles all over it. That didn't set too well with Uncle Gordon and I think that was one of the few times I got a whipping from someone other than my parents. I never shot any more windows after that.

**The barn we used for target practice**

85

**Cousin Joe Ketchie and Aunt Lib**

One day, Joe and I were having trouble finding
something to do and we started to argue a little bit. Arguing
in front of Uncle Gordon, while he was sitting on the porch
and resting in his rocking chair, was not a great idea. I think
it was a good possibility that we had interrupted his nap.
When Uncle Gordon heard us arguing, he just got up and
went inside the house. I thought to myself that we might be

in deep doo-doo, but Joe thought that we had just dodged another bullet.

When Uncle Gordon came out of the house, he was carrying two paddles that were made out of plywood. They were about twelve inches wide at the top and sported a nifty handle. Joe and I looked at each other and wondered if we were going to get a paddling with those things. I couldn't imagine why Uncle Gordon would need two different paddles unless he had gone into personalizing punishments. Then, he handed each of us a paddle. I looked at Joe, and Joe looked at me. We were wondering if we had to paddle each other.

**Grandma Ketchie's porch**

As it turned out, bumblebees had recently been swarming around the porch, and just about everybody, except Uncle Gordon, was afraid to come near it. He wasn't scared of much of anything. He reached over in the corner, picked up Grandma's broom, turned it upside down, and commenced to jabbing the ceiling of the porch with the handle.

There was now no doubt what we were to do with those paddles. The bumblebees were coming out from the porch ceiling by the hundreds and were headed straight for Joe and me. We started swatting those bees as fast as we could swat. You should have heard the sound those suckers made when they hit our paddles. We must have fought them off for a good fifteen minutes before our arms gave out. We were sweating like hogs, (I don't know if hogs sweat or not), when we finished, but we escaped without a single sting. We weakly retreated to the back yard to recover from the whole experience.

We finally got up enough nerve to carefully peek around the corner of the house and could see Uncle Gordon, peacefully napping in his rocking chair. We quietly made our way through the piles of dead bumblebees and tip-toed up to Joe's room for a little R & R. From then on, we never argued in front of Uncle Gordon and we never had trouble finding something to do.

There is another incident that readily stands out in my mind, even today. I have alluded to the fact that Aunt Lib was a fantastic cook and that I was a huge fan of her culinary abilities. One day, Joe and I went into the dining room and lifted the big cloth that covered the food, left over from dinner—just to see what was there. (We did that a lot.) I was always hungry. Well, lo and behold, there was this beautiful angel food cake that Aunt Lib had just taken out of the oven and placed under the cloth for safe-keeping.

It was just one of those spur-of-the-moment times in our lives when Joe and I looked at each other and made a snap decision. We simultaneously, grabbed hold of that cake, ripped it in half, and each of us took off out the back door carrying his hunk of heaven.

As you know, angel food cake is really soft and airy, so both Joe and I wadded our pieces into a tight ball, and ate them just like they were apples. It didn't seem like a whole lot of cake to me.

Wouldn't you know it? Aunt Lib had baked that thing especially for the ladies of the First Presbyterian Church who were coming to visit Grandma that afternoon. Talk about bad luck!

Aunt Lib went into the dining room to check on her beautiful cake only to find that it had gone missing; (So had Joe and I!) When Uncle Gordon finally found the two felonious members of the Ketchie family, he made sure that we would always remember that cake-stealing incident. I'll put it this way; I don't know about Joe, but I never stole another one of Aunt Lib's cakes. This was another time that I got a whipping from someone other than my parents. Those extra-curricular whippings always seemed to have involved Joe.

When Uncle Gordon got his new, rubber-tired wagon, the old wooden one was left to die an agonizingly, slow death. We kids just couldn't stand the thought of that. The old wagon had been resting between the horse trough and corncrib for many, many months. It just about broke our hearts to see it rotting away. Joe and I decided it should go out in a blaze of glory. He, Laura, and I pushed and pulled that cumbersome thing all the way down the lane and up to the top of the pasture hill. It was a monumental task! To tell you the truth, it was too much like work for me, but I persevered.

We finally got that old wagon situated right where we wanted it, in order to get the best ride that we possibly could. We figured it would be its last ride and wanted to make it a memorable one. Joe struggled with the heavy tongue of the wagon and finally got it positioned where he could use it to steer. He had to stand up on the frame to get any leverage. Laura and I tried to find a place to sit and hold on. The wagon frame was all that was remaining, so there wasn't any real good places to ride. We eventually considered ourselves as ready as we would ever be. I gave it a nudge, and we were off. I didn't have to run behind very long before I jumped up on to my assigned seat. Joe had a lot of trouble from the very beginning, trying to steer with the unyielding wagon tongue. The thing hadn't been greased for months and it was stuck! We were approaching the trees along the branch extremely fast and had to make a quick decision to go for it or abort our mission. Without taking a vote on the situation, we decided to abort. It must have been unanimous because we all jumped about the same time. It was a good thing, too; that old wagon hit the trees at top speed since it had picked up a great deal of momentum while rolling down the hill. I had never heard such a crash! Pieces of wooden spokes, rims, splinters, and I don't know what all, went flying through the air. The remainder of the wagon ended up in the branch at the bottom of the hill.

When we finally quit tumbling head over heels to the bottom of the hill, we were shocked to see such destruction. The old wagon had taken its last ride; and thank God, we had sense enough to jump off when we did. I had heard that God looks after ignorant people and drunks. Since we didn't drink, I figured we belonged in the other category. I suppose the wagon's remains are still there today. I do think we did it proud.

After the horses were sold, we didn't have any noble steeds on which to ride when we played like we were Roy Rogers, but we did have some milk cows. We would often climb up in the barn loft and make hideouts throughout the bales of hay. I guess we were like the "Hole in the Wall Gang", except our holes were tunnels through hay bales. I had an asthma attack almost every time I got around the barn loft. I had to play fast because I would have to go home soon after getting around that musty hay.

We would often wait patiently for the right moment to pull our Roy Rogers' stunt. Sure enough, one of Uncle Gordon's unsuspecting cows would wander right under the door of the loft. As a rule, cows are about as dumb as a bag of hammers and slow as Christmas. (I said, as a rule.) The way it usually went was something like this: I would make my jump, and the dumb cow would hear me and take off every time. I would either end up in a pile of manure after I took my daring leap or I would tear my britches on a nail. Neither one of the results was anything to brag about. To make matters worse, I still had to go home and face Mama. She had to do the washing and the patching of my clothes.

Such were the times when we were young and light of heart, but I was usually heavy in the butt.

# Springtime

Late February or early March welcomed the daffodils and colorful crocuses. We always called the daffodils buttercups. When we saw these hearty flowers, we knew that spring was not far behind.

Springtime in the South is a glorious time of the year. Red buds, yellow bells, dogwoods, and azaleas coat the countryside with a rainbow of colors.

Grandma had a great big row of beautiful, buttercups that bloomed along the driveway. I would pick a bouquet of the fragrant, bright-yellow flowers and take them to Mama. She always acted grateful and was pleased that her youngest offspring would be capable of such an act of kindness. She would put them in a jar of water and set them on the kitchen table. Their fragrance would fill the whole house. Her youngest son had already learned how to make points with his Mama. I never could get far enough ahead in the points department. I never knew when I was going to need some extra ones.

March was one of my favorite months in the springtime. Trees would be budding, the wind would be blowing, and we would play outside until dark.

Roger taught me how to make a homemade kite out of a piece of Blue Horse notebook paper and a couple pieces of broom sedge. He just slit the paper a little bit in each of the corners and in the center of the page. Then, he threaded the broom sedge through the slits crosswise and tied a piece of lightweight string to the place where they crossed—and that was that. The kite was really lightweight and would only fly in a soft, gentle breeze.

I bought a box-kite one time that was really fun to fly. It seemed to stay aloft effortlessly, so early one morning before I went to school, I ran down to the grass lot, launched it, and then tied its string to a stake I had driven into the ground. Would you believe it was still flying high when I got home from school that afternoon? I'm not making this stuff up; it really was!

I remember making a huge kite at grandma's house one day. She gave us a large piece of brown paper and some string, and we went to work on that thing right there on her sitting room floor. Roger cut the paper in the shape of a kite and then we laid the string around the edges of it. Next, we took some flour and water and made a paste to hold the string in place. Then the edges of the paper were folded across the string. There were gaps left at the corners where the string stuck out and notched reeds were fitted right onto the exposed string where the openings were. This made a real sturdy kite that was taller than I was. Grandma made the tail out of some old rags and we fastened it to the bottom of our giant homemade kite.

I remember the maiden voyage because the wind was so strong we could hardly hold onto that oversized flying creation. Roger was always a little ahead of the rest of us in the scientific department and figured that the size of the kite and the strength of the wind would require something stronger than the regular kite string that we usually used. He brought out some of Daddy's fishing line, tied it to the kite, and wrapped the other end around a big stick. He kept the kite real close to his body until we got it safely to the big grass lot behind Grandma's house.

The time finally arrived to launch it and Roger let me hold the kite while he controlled the string and stick. I didn't have to run with it or anything; I just held it up in the air and let it go. The huge kite took off so quickly in the strong wind, it started jerking Roger around. It was all he could do to just to hold on. The kite kept going and going and going. Before long, he sent me home to confiscate some more of

Daddy's fishing line. When I returned, he added the extra line to our kite and it kept on going higher and higher. That mega kite seemed really small as it gracefully flew hundreds of feet up in the March sky. Roger made me go back home one more time and steal some more of Daddy's line.

After adding the last batch of line, Roger finally let me hold onto the stick that controlled the kite. It now had well over five hundred yards or more of Daddy's fishing line attached to it. I could feel that giant kite tugging on the line, and it was difficult for me to control it, but Roger was tired and needed a break. I held on to the stick for a while, but soon the kite began pulling me across the grass lot, and I started hollering for help. Good ol' Roger—to the rescue as usual! He began winding all that fishing line back onto the stick. When the kite finally neared the ground, I grabbed on to the tail, and it lifted me off the ground like I was a mere child. (I suppose I was a mere child—wasn't I?) Anyway, that was a thrill! It was just about dark when we got home. What an experience!

Daddy would often take us for walks in the woods. He enjoyed showing us all the different kinds of trees and their blossoms, and teaching us to recognize each one of them. He thought learning stuff like that was extremely important, and he wanted us to learn everything about nature that we could. Well, Joe and I had already learned some interesting facts about nature from Aunt Ruth's *National Geographic* magazines. We had become well informed about the female anatomy in foreign countries. However, I'll have to admit I didn't know "bean dip" about trees.

We could hardly wait to go barefooted and looked forward to that "first time" each spring that we were allowed to go without our shoes on a regular basis. We weren't allowed to go barefooted until the dogwoods were blooming or bumblebees had been sighted. It didn't matter which one we saw first, just as long as we saw one or the other. We couldn't wait to tell Mama when we saw a bumblebee. She would believe just about anything we told her just to get us to shut up. She always said that I was the "water dripper" in the family. I guess a "water dripper" is someone that never stops annoying you. She was probably right—I never quit my "water dripping" until we had our shoes off for the season. It was like Heaven to go running through the fresh, green grass with the blades tickling our toes. One major drawback about this barefoot business was that we had to wash our feet every dad-gummed night.

There are a number of uncomfortable things that can happen to your feet when you run around everywhere without shoes. I remember stepping on lots of honeybees in the springtime. Those little buggers really took offense when you stepped on one of them and would retaliate with a sharp sting. I would hop around like I had been shot in the foot every time that happened to me.

We had to be really vigilant and watch where we stepped when we were walking around the farm. There were dogs, chickens, guineas, cows, and horses walking around the barnyard, too. It was a really an unpleasant feeling when you realized you had just stepped in something you wished you hadn't, and it was squashed between you toes.

Stepping on sharp objects was another hazard that often befell us barefooted kids. One day, Laura and I were playing in the driveway and she stepped on a piece of broken glass. Her foot was severely cut and blood was pouring out of the open wound. Mama and Daddy were not home, so she started hopping on the other foot toward Grandma's house.

Well, Mr. Malcolm heard her squalling like a banshee and came out of his back door too see what was happening. He saw her hopping on one foot while blood was pouring out of the other one. He finally convinced her to stop and let him look at the cut. He calmed her down a little bit and had me to help her stand while he got some kerosene from his car shed. That was not what Laura had in mind, I can tell you that. I thought Laura was going to lose it right there. Mr. Malcolm poured some kerosene on the wound and Laura commenced to hollering again. I don't think the kerosene hurt her—I think it was just the unknown variable that surprised her.

She pushed Mr. Malcolm out of her way and resumed her one-legged-hopping-trip all the way to Grandma's house where she would be bandaged deftly by the loving hands she sought. Laura was soon in a much better mood. If Grandma couldn't fix it, nobody could.


Springtime brought many wonderful opportunities for personal enrichment. Grandma's apple orchard was across the field that was right behind our house. She would often sit on her porch in the spring and summer months and could easily see when some interloper was invading her apple trees. She never had to wait very long to catch one of us kids roosting among the branches, raiding her trees.

Laura was undoubtedly the worst. She would sometimes pick apples off the trees while the blossoms were still attached. Grandma would invariably put her fingers in her mouth and let loose with one of her shrill whistles that you could hear for a country mile. We knew there was trouble when we heard her do that.

Sometimes she would just yell at us to get out of her apple trees. I think she was really worried that we would get a bellyache from eating so many green apples. I don't ever remember Laura or me having a green-apple-bellyache, and believe me, we ate plenty of them.

We always left plenty of apples for Aunt Lib to make her wonderful pies. We looked forward with great anticipation to the days she baked her fresh apple pies in their woodstove. She also would fry dried apple pies in an iron skillet. I think I liked them the best. You could just pick one of those suckers up in your hands and began eating it while you were still walking out the door. It didn't get any better than that! I thought I'd died and gone to Heaven when I got one of those things in my possession.


Springtime also brought other chores that were not necessary in the winter. Uncle Gordon kept several beehives near the orchard so that the honeybees would have plenty of convenient blossoms for making honey.

Robbing bees was always a big event for us kids. Daddy would help Uncle Gordon get suited up with the screen-wired-bonnet that Grandma had made for him to protect his face. Daddy would often help rob bees with nothing on but a pair of pants. He often went shirtless and shoeless in the warm months. Daddy would put some old rags in a bellowed-smoker and set them on fire. When the smoker got going really well, he would aim it at the bees that were clinging to the super. (That's the thing the honey is made on.) The smoke was supposed to make the bees lethargic and less aggressive. All that smoke would have made me mad as the dickens, if I had been a bee.

One afternoon, Daddy evidently got stung one time too many while helping Uncle Gordon rob bees. He began walking up the long driveway toward our house when he became really sick. He was crawling on his hands and knees by the time he got to our back door. Mama rushed him to the doctor where he learned that he was allergic to bee stings. The doctor told him that another sting could be fatal and for him to never go around the hives again. As far as I know, he never did.

The really good thing about robbing bees was that we got to eat all the fresh honey we could hold—right out of the dishpan. We would often eat honey until we got sick or had to spend the night in the bathroom.

Late spring and early summer would find us kids in the backyard trying to catch June Bugs. We would tie a piece of lightweight string around one of their legs and watch them fly around while we were holding on to the other end. It was kind of like having a remote control flying machine.

We also caught lightning bugs and put them in a jar. We would punch holes in the lid so they could live a long time, but they were usually given their freedom when we had to go to bed. Sometimes, I put lightning bugs in my mouth. It was really neat to find Mama and freak her out when I started talking. She would scream. "Take those nasty things out of your mouth, right this minute." (She always added right this minute for emphasis.) I can almost still taste those lightning bugs.

I remember one fine spring day when Mrs. Brawley's fourth grade class went on a field trip to Edmiston Dairy Farm in Rowan County to see how milk was bottled. Our family got our milk directly from the cows and kept it in a half-gallon Mason jar. I thought everybody did that. I think there were some girls on this trip that didn't realize milk came from cows. I guess they just thought it came from grocery stores.

I was the only kid in the whole class who didn't have any shoes on that day. When they took us into the "Cold Room" where the milk was stored, I wished I had some shoes on too. I kept jumping around, trying to keep my feet off that cold floor. It didn't work very well—one foot was always on the floor.

Freezing my bare feet off was worth it though, because we were each rewarded with a half-pint of their wonderful chocolate milk after the tour was over. I had to have help getting the stopper out of the bottle because I had bitten my fingernails off up to my elbows. I never could do that task by myself. It was a great trip, and I was really grateful for that chocolate milk.

I had always bitten my fingernails and sooner or later the shortness of them became a problem. There were just some things I could not accomplish because of my nail-biting habit.

When I was in the third grade, Mrs. Jewel Brown, our teacher, would always have to help me get that confounded stopper out of my milk bottle at lunchtime. One day, she decided that she had had enough of doing that "stopper thing" for me everyday, and showed me how to take my fork and stick it under the tab and lift it up. She was so proud of her acumen for opening milk bottles. It sounded real good in principle, but I was no "mental giant", folks.

Showing me how to do this for myself was Mrs. Brown's first mistake. Then, she remained right beside me to be sure that I was doing this complicated task as per her instructions. That was her second mistake! I promptly pushed down with the fork instead of lifting up. The stopper went to the bottom of the bottle, and the milk went to the top of Mrs. Brown's head. She wore these little, rimless glasses and; all of a sudden, they were white. Her hair was white, too. You would never have thought that just a little half-pint of milk could do so much damage to a third-grade schoolteacher. The whole class was truly amazed but didn't say a word. You know what? She helped me get my milk open for the remainder of the third grade. I don't know what made her change her mind.

Daddy and Mama were always getting on my case and Laura's, too; telling us that biting our fingernails was not good for us. I didn't know why it wasn't—fingernails didn't make you fat, give you bad breath, or make your stomach hurt. Somebody that was educated beyond their intelligence had told them that biting your fingernails would give you appendicitis.

Well, when I was nine years old, I had to stay home from school because I had a really high fever. Mama had Dr. Mac Henderson come to our house to see me. (Doctors made house calls in those days!) I was lying on the couch, minding my own business and feeling really miserable, when he started poking on me. I just about jumped off the couch when he poked down below my belly. He had me admitted to the hospital that evening, and I was operated on later that night for appendicitis. They never did tell me if my appendix was full of fingernails, so I didn't see any reason to stop biting them after the operation. I didn't have an appendix to harm any more and I had to do something with my nervous energy, so I resumed my nail biting.

I gave up the nail-biting habit later in life after everybody quit trying to make me stop. Stubborn cuss, wasn't, I?

So goes the life of country kids in the springtime.

# Ice Cold Watermelon

Ice cold watermelon was one of my favorite treats during the "Dog Days" of summer. We always planted a few watermelons, but they rarely lived up to our great expectations. We did, however, know who raised the biggest and best watermelons anywhere around and they were either related to us or lived close by.

I vividly remember an incident that took place in my life when I was nine or ten years old. (I would just as soon forget it, but the memory of the indiscretion keeps creeping up on me when I least expect it.) One day, I stealthily sneaked into Uncle Frank's watermelon patch. He had some of the biggest watermelons I had ever seen. I had been watching them grow all summer and already had one picked out. I felt that it truly belonged to me. After all, I'm the one who had been coveting that watermelon for months. I figured loyalty alone ought to be worth something. That watermelon was so big that I couldn't even lift it off the ground. I definitely couldn't eat it out in the open patch where Uncle Frank or Aunt Ella might see me commit the heinous crime. I was in a real quandary.

I never was a rocket scientist and didn't know much about physics, but I figured that I could roll that sucker through Uncle Frank's little patch of woods and hide it behind Grandma's barn in the haystack. That worked real well, but by the time I accomplished all the manual labor, it was late, and I had to go home. I thought about that beautiful watermelon all night and was hoping it was cooling in the shade of the haystack and would be ready for our rendezvous the next day.

The next day dawned clear and warm. Daddy kept finding stuff for me to do all morning, and I knew he would be suspicious if I declined dinner. Dinner was always at 12:00 noon at our house. I ate as much as usual so I wouldn't draw attention to myself due to a lack of appetite—I was always hungrier than a woodpecker with a headache. I finally escaped the bonds of slavery and made a "beeline" for the haystack.

I knew I had a major dilemma on my hands when I couldn't find the purloined watermelon where I left it in the haystack the day before. Somebody was in big trouble, and I prayed it wasn't me.

Wouldn't you know, Daddy had been visiting Grandma the day before! While sitting on her corner porch, he had witnessed his youngest son rolling a big watermelon out of the woods, through Uncle Gordon's garden and toward the back of the barn.

He had already informed Uncle Frank of the egregious crime that his youngest offspring had committed. Daddy thought that it would be in my best interest if I would own up to the incident or face serious consequences.

I then had the unpleasant task of knocking on Uncle Frank's door and confessing my dastardly deed. He just laughed when I admitted my transgression and told me to go look behind the haystack. Daddy had moved the stolen watermelon—he wanted me to sweat a little bit, and it really worked. I ate part of the stolen goods, but I didn't enjoy it nearly as much as I thought I would.

Later, Uncle Frank told me that I was welcome to have a watermelon any time I wanted one but to be sure to ask him first. I didn't have a problem with that; so I readily agreed. I really learned a valuable lesson thanks to that nefarious act of indiscretion. Honesty is the best policy—I ate a ton of his watermelons after that and had no guilty conscience.

Mr. John Neill's watermelon patch was about a mile or so from our house. Traversing through the woods and pastures for such a great distance; made it impossible for me to bring one of those heavy treasures back home. Mr. Neill was known for raising whoppers on his bottomland property— some grew to gigantic proportions!

We had given Mr. Neill advanced warning that we were about to invade his patch. He didn't just have a patch; he had a doggoned watermelon field. I never saw so many watermelons in one place in my life. We ran around that field, thumping and thumping, trying to find the ripe ones. I finally chose a big, striped one and had to roll it all the way to the creek because I couldn't pick the thing up. It probably weighed forty pounds.

I just sat down in the creek with my watermelon between my legs and let the cool water run over us. It was hard work, manipulating that giant member of the melon family all the way to the water. I hit that prized melon as hard as I could with my fist a couple of times and "busted" it wide open. I began scooping that wonderful, red, juicy, dripping stuff into my mouth as fast as I could and politely spitting the seeds into the running water. I didn't want to make a mess. It was really convenient eating in the creek—I just washed off right where I sat. Mr. Neill was an extremely nice man and we really appreciated his generosity and his big, juicy watermelons.

Uncle Gordon grew some big ones, too, but I don't think he trusted us boys because he didn't leave them in the patch very long. He would load his watermelons in a trailer and take them to the shed behind their house where he could keep an eye on them.

He had a big milk-cooler in the shed that kept the water temperature just right for their ten-gallon milk cans. The temperature was also just right for Uncle Gordon's big watermelons. I loved to go behind Grandma's back porch to the shed where the cooler was and lift the lid just to see what Uncle Gordon was hiding. It was a beautiful sight to see those big, striped watermelons floating in that icy water. They would get so cold that when you cut one; it would make a cracking sound when the halves began separating. I never heard anything more pleasant than that sound. Those things tasted so good it almost made my teeth hurt.

Carl Harkey owned and operated the old Oak Grove Service Station and Grocery Store less than a half-mile north of our house. I would often walk the railroad track to his store. Sometimes I would walk on one of the rails all the way, without falling off. I usually bragged about it when I arrived at the store, but half the time, nobody believed me.

Most times, I would either walk up the highway or ride my bicycle. Sometimes I would carry a foot tub with me when I walked and pick up bottles on the way. All soft drinks came in glass bottles back then and Carl would pay me three cents for each bottle—that added up quickly. I usually had picked up enough bottles by the time I got to the store to buy an RC Cola and a Moon Pie with the deposit money I got from the bottles. The RC and Moon Pie together only cost about fifteen cents. I still like Moon Pies, especially the Double Decker ones, but they have too many "carbs" for me now, since I developed diabetes several years ago.

Carl always sold a lot of watermelons in the summertime. The gas pumps were located under a large roof that extended out from the store. It was always shady and cool under there, and that is where huge stacks of those summertime delicacies were kept. (Nobody likes a hot watermelon.) When the watermelon sales were real slow, Carl got worried that he would lose a lot of money on them. Watermelons didn't keep very long. (Carl hated to lose money.) Being the astute businessman and marketing expert that he was, he would have some of us boys take off our shirts and eat watermelons while the juice ran down our bellies. This marvelous example of marketing genius took place right in front of that huge stack of melons. This task was always performed with great alacrity, (that's enthusiasm, for the unenlightened). After seeing this visual display of pure satisfaction on the faces of us poor, country boys, the potential customers could not resist buying at least one.

I have noticed that many of my childhood memories often have something to do with food. I still like watermelons, too.

# All Kinds of Fishing

We always played, hunted, and fished in somebody's pastures or woods—Grandma's, Uncle Frank's, or Robert Oliphant's—it didn't make a whole lot of difference to us. We really enjoyed fishing for minnows in the little branches that ran through their properties. The streams always had lots of minnows or their bigger cousins, "hornyheads", swimming around everywhere, just begging to be caught.

We would bend a straight pin into a crooked angle, tie it to a piece of string, fasten the string to an old stick, and we were in business. It wasn't major fishing tackle, but it worked really well for us. All we needed were some worms, and they were plentiful. We just dug some up and took off for the pasture.

I will have to admit that the fishing was a little better at Robert Oliphant's. The fishing holes were a little bigger and a little deeper. Therefore the fish were a little bigger. We just threw the worm-loaded straight pin into the water, and pretty soon a minnow would grab it and take off. You had to pull it out fast, or he would get away because there was no barb on the pin to hold the minnow on. They were fast little rascals, too. We actually called them "minners".

When we wanted to do some serious fishing for minnows, we would make a little seine out of some old wire or a fertilizer sack that we found lying around somewhere. Sometimes we took those poor, little fish and used them for bait to catch some bigger fish in the Catawba River. A tasty, Catawba catfish was good eating for a hungry boy. As a rule, we just caught minnows for fun and let them loose to swim in our hallowed streams another day.

When the fishing was slow, we would often find a grapevine hanging from a lofty limb and pretend we were

Tarzan as we swung out across the stream while yelling like crazy. We practiced our best Tarzan yells, but they never came out quite right. Sometimes our yelling would start the dogs barking and howling, but I really didn't think that our impersonation of Tarzan was all that bad.

The vines also had the bad habit of breaking at inopportune times sending us crashing into the water. Some grapevine swings lasted a good year or so before we subdued them into uselessness. The more we swung on them, the more they stretched, and the lower they hung, until finally our butts were dragging the ground during take-off. We knew then it was time to find another one to conquer.

Before we could do any serious fishing for catfish, we had to have some bait. Daddy would often take me with him to some of the small branches near our house. Daddy thought that branch grubs were some of the best bait to use for catching catfish. Who was I to argue? He was the fishing expert. I just never figured out why we had to do this grubbing thing in March. It was cold work—stooping down in the little streams and turning over the dead leaves under the water. Sometimes, my hands would seem like they were freezing. When those branch grubs started rolling up from under the leaves and began floating down stream, we just picked them out of the water and dropped them into a bucket. Daddy had already prepared the bucket with old, wet leaves. The grubs never complained about their new home; so I guess they were satisfied.

Daddy also liked to use hellgrammites for bait. Those awful, squiggly things came equipped with a set of painful pinchers on them, and they knew how to use them, too. I hated to bait my hook with one of them. They would grip one of my fingers with their pincers and hold on until it would bleed. Boy, those things hurt like the devil! They were great for catching catfish, though. We would head for the foothills or the mountains to catch those nasty things. It would often be early spring when Daddy decided it was time to hit the icy waters. It looked to me like they would live there all year long. Where else were they going to go? It wasn't so bad when we went wading in search of these illusive, little monsters in July. March was quite another story. We had a piece of screen wire that we set downstream from where we stirred the riverbed with a hoe. This would run those nasty hellgrammites right into our screen, so we could just pick them up and drop them into a bucket. You had to be extremely careful when you were picking them up, or you got pinched every time.

David Wilson went with us fishing most of the time and he really enjoyed getting in the water and digging around for hellgrammites. I usually helped hold the screen to capture the elusive devils but often relinquished the picking-them-up-job to Daddy.

**Gathering hellgrammites in a cold mountain stream**

Daddy took fishing about as seriously as anyone did. He absolutely loved it. He kept a couple of old Pflueger reels oiled up and ready to go. He and Mr. Bruce Gillespie would take off in Daddy's old, red Ford pickup truck and go just

106

about anywhere there was a chance of kidnapping a fish from its watery home and bringing it to our house for supper.

One Sunday we were at Daniel Boone's Cave on the banks of the Yadkin River, and Daddy couldn't pass up a chance to throw a hook in the water. He asked me to climb all the way back up the steep hill to the car and bring him his fishing stuff. I, being the obedient son that I was, returned with it—post haste. He baited up and cast out into the flowing Yadkin. It looked as though it would be a good day to catch some nice catfish. It rained the night before, and the water was perfect. He didn't have the hook in the water for ten minutes when he started reeling it in. I asked him, "What's the matter?"

He just kept reeling then gathered all the gear back up and said, "Let's go."

I couldn't believe it. On the way back up that big hill, he told me, "I just can't fish on Sunday." He meant it, too. I realized then that living a godly life was more important to him than fishing. It was a lesson that I have never forgotten. I may not have always adhered to it, but I have never forgotten it.

**Daddy fishing on Sunday**

We fished an awful lot in the old Catawba River. Daddy always said that the Blue Catawba Cats were the best catfish there were. (I never did see a blue catfish.) But, who was I to argue? I ate them like there was no tomorrow.

**A good day of fishing with Daddy**

Sometimes when we went fishing, it would be so cold I would beg him to let me build a fire. I think he thought the fish would see the blaze, be wary, and not bite his hook. I told you he took fishing seriously. Once in a while, he would succumb to my entreaty just to get me to shut up. (He thought the fish could <u>hear</u> us, too.) I remember one night, begging him to quit fishing and take my freezing, little butt home. I was afraid I would be found right there the next morning—frozen to the bait bucket on which I had been sitting for the past four or five hours. He kept saying, "I'm just fixin' to get a bite. I can tell he's almost ready. Wait just one more minute." This would go on for another hour or so and I would still be sitting there without a fire. You had to admire his faith. He had his faith, and I had mine, but I used mine praying for a fire.

Several families went in together and purchased a huge, sixty-foot drag seine. We were getting real serious about catching some major catfish out of the old Catawba River. The seine had to be fitted and hung properly, and the only man that could do that was Mr. Hamp Bailey who lived on Bailey Road, just off Highway 21 North. Mr. Hamp was an older fellow. He had a big, beautiful mustache that I just couldn't help but admire. I saw a picture of Mark Twain once, and he had a mustache just like Mr. Hamp's. Since I only knew Mr. Hamp and had not met Mark Twain personally, I didn't know who had theirs first. I had never seen a mustache that impressive before, except in books and most of them were on some dead people who lived a long time ago. Mr. Hamp and his mustache lived with George Bailey and his family. George and I have been friends since the first grade, and Mr. Hamp was his grandpa.

We unloaded the seine and spread it out across the Bailey's front yard, under a big, water oak tree. Mr. Bailey started sewing a big chain across part of the seine to weight the bottom so the seine would stay as close to the riverbed as possible. This kept the fish from swimming under it. He then attached each end of the seine to staffs that Uncle Gordon made out of some Hickory saplings. The top of the seine would then be fitted with some cork floats to keep the top at water level. Everything had a purpose when it came to hanging a seine. What a sight it was when they stretched it out in its full glory and laid it on the green grass. I knew we were in for some major fun and, later on, major eating.

A bunch of us would pile into a couple of old cars and head for the Catawba River. The seine was usually loaded into the trunk of Jay Neill's old '41 Ford. We had a car squashed full with Jay, his brother Bill and his two sons Larry and Dwight, Roger, Daddy, and me. (We didn't have to worry about seat belts back then.)The rest of the neighborhood would come along in the other car. It was quite an expedition.

Sometimes we would start several miles north of Highway 150 at East Monbo, fish both sides of Neill's Island, and work down the river toward Sherrill's Ford.

We would set the seine up along the bank of the river to trap anything we might scare out of their hiding places. Dwight, Larry, Roger, and I were then instructed to thrust our feet and legs up under the bank, while holding onto overhead limbs, and kick like crazy. This would run the fish—or whatever else was hiding under there—out into the seine. I suppose we were the chosen ones because of our age—I'm not really sure.

Large-mouth bass, perch, suckers, snakes, carp, turtles, and the prized "Catawba Cats" would flee the safety of their holes under the bank and swim right into our waiting net. The staffs would then be brought together and everyone would take their positions around the seine. We all had our jobs to do, and we knew what they were. We younger guys had to dive under the water and carefully keep the chains dragging the bottom and bring them together. We would take up the bottom of the seine with both chains safely held in our hands, while the top was gathered together by the other team. Then, with a team on the staffs, it would be lifted out of the water. Fish would be flopping everywhere; it was just like Christmas. We had to throw the large-mouth bass and perch back in the water because it was against the law to catch them while seining. The catfish would promptly be thrown into a big fertilizer sack that was kept in the possession of one of us trustworthy youths. Nobody wanted the carp and suckers, so they were thrown back into the river, too. Snakes and turtles were allowed to escape unharmed.

One year, there was a huge thunderstorm upstream; and suddenly, torrents of raging, muddy water started rising so rapidly that we were helplessly caught on the west side of the river. We made our way down stream as best we could, while holding on to tree branches and toting sacks full of fish and the huge seine. It was not an easy task, and it was also very dangerous. The water was moving really fast and was now so deep we couldn't touch the bottom. We had parked on the east side of the river at East Monbo, which is in Iredell County, and this was a problem. We had to get out of the raging water before we drowned, but exiting the river on the west side meant we would be in Catawba County—we had a license to seine in Iredell and Mecklenburg Counties, but we didn't have one for Catawba County. We had a couple hundred pounds of catfish that we couldn't prove were caught in Iredell County. If we were caught, we would have been fined heavily and the seine confiscated. We didn't want that!

We all got out safely and hid with the seine and sacks full of catfish under a little bridge while we decided what to do. Daddy volunteered to swim across the swollen river and try to make it to the other side before reaching the dangerous rapids at Sherrill's Ford. We all watched him while praying he would make it safely. He barely made it across the turbulent river before the rapids and then had to walk several miles back to East Monbo to get one of our cars. This took a long time, and we were scared we were going to get caught with the illegal fish and seine.

Daddy drove Jay's old Ford all the way down Perth Church Road to Highway 150 and crossed the river into Catawba County. He then had to find the graveled road that led to the bridge where we were still in hiding. It was a huge relief to see Daddy driving up in that old Ford. All of us piled into the car on top of each other. We ended up with about ten or eleven people jammed into that old car with two hundred pounds of flopping catfish and a huge, wet seine piled in the trunk. We were low to the ground to say the least. We still had to drive all the way back up to East

Monbo and get the other car. We were not a pretty sight when we got home, but we had a huge mess of fish.

In Mecklenburg County, we usually seined the Horse Hole, Buzzard's Roost, Log Hole, and Burton's Deep Water—all located above the old, steel bridge at Beattie's Ford. The fishing was usually good at any of those spots.

We would often set the seine around big rocks and gravel for catfish. Graveling for catfish amounted to putting you hands under a rock and letting the fish nibble on your fingers until you could get a good hold of it and pull it out of its watery home. It was against the law to gravel without a seine.

I remember one time Jim Settlemyre pulled a big, snapping turtle out from under a rock. I retired from graveling that day! I used to put my hands under there, too, and feel the catfish nibbling on my fingers. After seeing Jim pull out turtles (and snakes, too) I thought my time would be better spent holding the sack.

Laura started dating a young man named Harold Cline about 1956 or so. He was a few years older than I, but still took me fishing with him fairly often, and we became best friends. His specialty was fishing for carp in stocked lakes. Harold made his own bait and was very adept at this carp fishing stuff. I went with him one day to Earnhardt's Lake in Cabarrus County and Harold baited my hook with some of his special mixture that only he knew the recipe for making. Let me tell you right now, I caught the biggest fish I have ever caught, thanks to Harold Cline. It weighed fifteen pounds and fourteen ounces. If you don't believe it, look at my picture. (See picture on next page.)

I will always be indebted to Harold for his friendship and patience. He, and my good friend, Bob Edmiston were co-owners of The Aisle Pawn Shop, right next to my gallery, on Main Street in Downtown Mooresville. Harold passed away recently and his passing has left a void in all of our lives. Bob still comes to work everyday and we are still great friends, but we never fish. Who has time?

**My prized fish**

There are countless stories and memories about my time spent fishing. There are too many to tell here, but all of them are special to me—some are pure treasures.

# Summer Garden and Canning

Mama would come home from work about 3:30 in the afternoon and check to see if we had all the work done. More often than not, it wouldn't be finished and without fail, she would always say, "I can't do everything and go to the mill, too." You could depend on her saying that every single time.

Daddy was unable to have a regular job for very long because of acute back pain. He broke his ankle in World War II, and it was not set correctly. This led to a problem with his knee and, eventually caused his back pain. He received a whopping $22 a month from the government for his disability. The Veteran's Administration did, however, buy him some Craftsman tools for a woodworking shop, and he began building outdoor furniture to sell. He made chaise lounges, Adirondack chairs, swings, etc. He was really good at it, but he never sold a whole lot so he ended up raising a vegetable garden and us kids. I think Daddy got the worst end of the deal. God granted Daddy a great amount of forbearance to use in raising his children. I think the good Lord had that in mind when He put Mama and Daddy together. Mama had a significant forbearance deficiency.

Our huge garden was located across the Statesville Highway in front of our house. It lay between the busy highway and the railroad track. The garden started in front of Mr. Blackwelder's and went all the way up to Aunt Lil Patten's driveway. That was way over a hundred yards—and more! We're talking a major garden, here. Daddy planted just about anything he thought we would eat and a few things he hoped we would. He was a man of great faith.

We had rows and rows of green beans, potatoes, tomatoes, radishes, sugar peas, and cabbage. We usually planted a couple of rows of onions and lima beans and at least one long row of cucumbers. We had some squash, too. Daddy believed that six or seven hills of squash would feed Iredell County if they were picked off every day.

The main section of the garden was in front of our house and went a little past Mr. Malcolm's. This is where the State of North Carolina erected a sign, smack-dab between the cucumbers and cabbage. It proclaimed that the state of North Carolina's right-of-way extended from the white line in the middle of Statesville Highway to the middle of our garden. The sign had a bunch of writing explaining all of that, and then there were some initials at the bottom: S H & P W C in big letters. Being the young and inquisitive boy that I was, I always wondered what those letters meant. A very reliable source, in the person of my big brother, informed me that the initials stood for "Shit Hooks and Poor Working Convicts". I learned later that it was actually, "State Highway and Public Works Commission". I thought the first interpretation had a much better ring to it. Roger rarely passed up an opportunity to enlighten his little brother.

Then there were the rows and rows of corn that ran all the way past Aunt Lil's driveway. Beneath the corn, we would grow black-eyed peas. You would think we did this gardening stuff for a living. We didn't, though! We ate just about everything we raised and then some. We were a hungry bunch of people. Daddy always said that we could eat the legs off the table.

I vividly remember walking across the road to the garden with Daddy one morning after a week of steady rain. He was standing there with a foot tub in his hand, looking over all the rows and said, "God at the glory vines." Morning Glories had invaded our garden and covered just about everything. Like I said before, Daddy was a man of faith. He had us start with one row at a time until we had it all cleaned and weeded again. It took us a few days, but we did it!

We plowed our garden with Old Bill. Bill was Uncle Gordon's mule and was as ornery as could be. I never could get that sucker to stay within the rows like a good mule should. I was a lightweight and couldn't handle him at all. I would plow up the plants instead of plowing in between the rows. It didn't take too much of this until Daddy would take over the reins. Then he would make me start hoeing the rows by hand. Maybe messing up the plowing wasn't such a good idea after all.

We had a ton of Bermuda grass in the garden that came from God-knows-where. We called it cane grass. Whatever the nasty stuff was, it was virtually impossible to kill. We dug it up, strand by strand, shook all the dirt from the roots, and threw it onto the railroad track. In a week it would be flourishing between the rocks and the crossties. I think that was really the grass from hell. It remained our bane throughout my childhood. It even sneaked across the highway and invaded our yard, too.

We didn't have a power mower, and the old, reel-type, push- mower we had was no match for that tough and wiry cane grass. We would have to get a running start to attack that stuff, only to be stalled in a few feet and have to try it again. Often, we staked our little bull calf in the yard to help keep the grass thinned down. That worked pretty well, but he would make the yard lumpy where he did his business. I don't know which was worse—mowing, or having a lumpy yard.

I don't know exactly why God, being all knowing and everything, made all of the garden stuff grow so close to the ground. It was the constant bending over part that I hated—it hurt my back. I was a chronic complainer and whiner when it came to working in the garden. I can still hear Daddy yell from across the highway, "Bow down! I don't want to see nothin' but your hind end and your elbows."

Daddy wasn't mean or anything like that; he just wanted me to do my job. I just didn't care for the job he had chosen for me to do. I felt that this gardening stuff would not be a good career choice for my future. I didn't know what I wanted to do when I grew up, but I did know that gardening was not in my top ten choices.

We had to carry buckets of water from the pump house in our backyard all the way across the Statesville Highway to water the plants—just to keep the garden growing. Work, work, work! After all the planting, nurturing, weeding, hoeing, and watering were done, then the danged stuff had to be picked. I didn't know which was worse. At least you could stand up while you hoed. I'll say it again; it was that bending over part that I hated!

Well, finally the day would come and the vegetables would be ripening. Sometimes I would go to the garden and pull a radish up out of the ground, wipe it on my pants, and eat it right there. I seemed to want something to eat just about all the time.

When the first big, juicy, ripe tomato was hanging on the vine, I would pull that sucker off and run to the house; smear some Duke's Mayonnaise on some light bread and make me a "mater sammage". You talk about gooooood! We ate tomato sandwiches all summer.

Inevitably the day would arrive when Daddy informed us that canning tomatoes was our next project. All of the doggoned things seemed to ripen at about the same time. We would pick buckets and buckets full of tomatoes and have to carry them all the way from the garden, across the highway, and around the house to the back porch. This is where I remember the serious tomato peeling being done. We peeled so many of the things that we got tired of seeing tomatoes, and we didn't care if we had any canned ones or not. I hated peeling tomatoes just as badly as the next person, but this one time—if you can believe it—I kept my mouth shut. Everyone was getting a little touchy.

I remember Laura whining so much about peeling tomatoes that Daddy finally told her that, if she said another word about it, she would be in big trouble. Laura was a lot like me—she just couldn't help herself. She said she was not going to peel any more tomatoes, and before any of us could even think, Daddy took the over-ripe, juicy "mater" he was peeling and threw that dripping thing at Laura and hit her squarely in the face. He couldn't help himself, either. It was so funny seeing Laura sitting there with the red juice running down her face, I couldn't help myself, either, and started laughing so hard I fell off my stool. That started Roger laughing, too; and Daddy couldn't help himself anymore and joined in. Laura even started laughing as she was wiping the juice off her face. She knew she had messed up! That was truly an episode of "not being able to help ourselves" if I ever saw one.

The laughter was really needed, and we all chipped in and worked harder than before and finished peeling the tomatoes before Mama got home from work. The tomato-throwing incident was never mentioned to Mama. We had to start the canning process next. It was really late when we finally got to bed. However, Laura never did think that "the tomato-in-the-face" episode was as funny as we did. I think she just laughed to keep from crying.

It took hundreds of Mason jars to fill the needs of the canning season. We canned pickles, tomatoes, green beans, jellies and jams, and a whole lot of other things I have forgotten. My chief job was to wash those blasted jars. You know, I liked that! We would have hundreds of jars drying all over the place. We never seemed to have enough extra money left over to buy canning jars. We often retrieved old jars from Mr. Lackey's trash gully and carried them home in a fertilizer sack. When they were boiled and washed up real good, you never knew the difference. As far as I know, nobody ever died because we used the jars we salvaged from the gully.

I remember one extremely hot, summer day when Daddy wanted us to gather some corn and get it ready for the freezer. It was so hot that day, I saw a dog chasing a rabbit toward the garden, and they were both walking. God, it was hot! All we wanted to do was go swimming. Daddy told Roger to go get one more sack full, and then we could quit for the day. I think he had already told Roger that same thing about a sack or two ago, and it made Roger kind of mad. Roger went down to those long, long rows of corn and picked every, single, solitary ear of corn he could find. It took seven trips back to the corn patch and seven wheelbarrow loads just to bring it all to the house. Well, I'll tell you right now, Laura and I were not happy with Roger about the whole situation.

Mama got home from work around 3:30 and saw the sacks full of corn lying all over the yard and said the expected, "I can't do everything and go to the mill, too." We started shucking and silking that stuff and got madder and madder. Laura and I started smashing down on some of the juicy kernels of corn and squirting the juice on each other and things just got worse. By the time the corn was ready for freezing, we were throwing it at each other. We were all a bunch of very weary corn shuckers. We were still putting up corn at 2:30 in the morning and I was then, too tired to get my beauty sleep. Maybe that incident was the reason I didn't turn out any better looking than I did. Roger outdid himself on that one. It was not one of his better days, and I'm still trying to forgive him for it.

I always trusted my daddy and believed anything he told me would be the truth. I also trusted his acumen pertaining to insects and other creatures of nature. Well, there was this one incident, in the gardening annals of this little white-headed boy; that left me questioning the soundness of his judgment.

I was helping Daddy in the garden one July day by cutting okra off the stalks and putting the pods in my bucket like a good little boy should, when out of the blue a bumblebee seemed to be attracted to me. I never have claimed to be a big bumblebee fan and I guess this particular bee took umbrage with the fact.

The bee circled my head a few times and looked as if he was looking for somewhere to light. I did not desire to be his landing place and started jumping around so he wouldn't have a chance to take advantage of my youth and inexperience.

Well, Daddy being the man of great faith that he was, told me to just be still and the bumblebee wouldn't bother me. I don't know if you have ever had a bumblebee swarming around your head looking for a place to light or not, but I have, and I didn't want to be still. Daddy finally said, "Trust me on this, son. Don't move and he will fly away and leave you alone."

Just this one time, I did as I was instructed. That danged bumblebee circled a few more times and lit right on the end of my nose. I broke out in a sweat, watching him with crossed-eyes, as he perched on the end of my proboscis.

"Help!" I begged.

Daddy said once again, "Don't move and he will leave you alone."

I was too scared to move and stood as still as a statue with sweat or something running down my legs. Undoubtedly, bees don't acknowledge the same "standing still" rule in which Daddy had so much faith. That sucker stung me so hard on the end of my nose that I thought I'd die right there on the spot. You can bet your sweet life that I didn't stay still any longer. I started squalling and left the garden post-haste with Daddy staring at his youngest son kicking up a dust trail through the rows of okra.

My poor nose swelled up so big that I looked like Jimmy Durante. I didn't go out of the house for a few days because I didn't want anyone looking at me while I was still in my abnormal condition. I really appreciated the fact that Roger and Laura didn't make too much fun of my unfortunate encounter with the bumblebee. I think they realized that it could have been one of them, instead of me, that had the same misfortune. The swelling eventually went down and everything got back to normal.

I know Daddy didn't intend to give me bad advice, but I never stood still any more if there was a big bumblebee involved. It was about this time in my life that I began questioning the wisdom of some of my daddy's logic.

I will always remember the year we had a "bumper" potato crop. Daddy had always planted by the "Signs"—the ones he found in Blum's Almanac. Uncle Gordon would laugh at him for this and tell Daddy that it was just a bunch of superstition. That particular year, Uncle Gordon planted his potatoes at what seemed like the perfect time for planting potatoes. Daddy waited for a few weeks, and Uncle Gordon kept reminding him to plant our potatoes real soon or we were not going to have any to eat during the winter. Uncle Gordon's potato plants grew and grew and were really beautiful. They had pretty blooms all over the huge vines. He was so proud. We finally planted ours when Daddy said the signs were right, but our plants never caught up with Uncle Gordon's.

I still remember helping Uncle Gordon, Aunt Lib, and Joe take up their potato crop that year. Old Bill was in rare form, and the soil was turning up real nice and pretty, but the potatoes were few and far between. They hardly got any potatoes at all! Uncle Gordon just kept shaking his head and wondering what happened.

Later, Joe came up to our house and helped us take up our crop. Joe couldn't believe it. Daddy had Old Bill turning the dirt, and those pretty potatoes were rolling out of the ground by the bushels! We ended up keeping Uncle Gordon's family in potatoes all winter, and we still had plenty for ourselves. I can't explain any of it. That was just the way it was.

When we got the potatoes loaded in five-gallon buckets, we carried them to the basement, where we spread them out on newspapers across a ledge. They would remain there until Mama would send one of us children to get some for supper.

We were making "Thirteen Day Pickles" one time, and Daddy was not too good at following directions. About the third day, we had to take the little bag of special spices out of the crock and do something to the cucumbers. After doing whatever it was we were supposed to do; Daddy told me to take the bag of spices and throw it in the incinerator where we burned our trash. I did that, being the good son I was. Well, he kept reading the directions and got a little farther along to where it said to put the little bag of spices back in the crock along with the pickles. Daddy said, "Son, go get them spices back." I ran out to the incinerator and got the bag of spices out of the ashes and handed it to Daddy. He washed the bag off under the spigot and put it back in the pickle crock. I never could tell that it hurt the flavor, and nobody ever died from that, either—as far as I know.

One extremely hot, August day, I remember we were making grape jelly and the temperature reached 104° in the shade. We were cooking the grapes in the kitchen, and it was probably 120° or more in there. We couldn't get the stuff to gel and couldn't figure out what the problem was. Every time some perplexing problem, to which Daddy didn't know the answer, would arise, he would send one of us kids hot-footin' it to Grandma's. Grandma knew just about everything about everything. She told us to put it all in the refrigerator because it was too hot for it to gel. Well, we never heard of such a thing. We were flying by the seat of our pants on this jelly making business. (We flew by the seat of our pants a lot while Mama worked in the mill.) Putting it in the refrigerator did the trick, and we had plenty of good grape jelly for the winter.

Gardening and canning were major events for us every summer and were necessary if we were going to eat very well in the winter. There were some good memories that went along with the hard work, but for some reason, I mostly remember the hard work.

# Harvesting Grain

Grandma's small farm didn't bring in enough money for them to buy the necessary harvesting equipment. John Brantley had just about any kind of machinery needed to harvest our crops, so he was the designated reaper. He had a big dusty-orange, Allis-Chalmers combine that he pulled behind his dusty-orange Allis-Chalmers tractor. He would drive them all the way over from his farm on Highway 21 and help us out. John was about the best there was, when it had anything to do with driving a tractor. He could manipulate that combine around the corners of the fields effortlessly, hardly ever leaving any uncut grain.

A combine was a pretty complicated piece of machinery. It had to be pulled alongside the tractor as its mowing machine blades cut about a five-foot swath of grain at a time. Then, the grain, stalks and all, were taken by a conveyer belt to a part of the machine that would separate the grain from the stalk. Then the grains would come down a pipe where two sacks were fastened and ready to be filled. When one sack was filled, someone had to remove it, tie a miller's knot around the top, and then put the sack on a chute that led to the ground. The remainder of the stalks were cut into smaller pieces and blown onto a spinning contraption that spread it across the field. The cut-up stalks were later baled for straw and used to spread on the stable floors.

Roger or Joe usually rode the combine and tied the sacks after they were filled with whatever grain we were harvesting at the time. Sometimes I rode with one of them and pushed the sacks down the short chute to the ground. I was not much use for anything else until it came time to load the sacks on the wagon. Wheat weighed sixty pounds to the bushel, barley weighed forty-eight pounds, and oats weighed thirty-four pounds. I couldn't handle two bushels of wheat or barley by myself. Someone usually helped me lift them onto the wagon. I was too light in the butt for heavy work.

Today, combines are self-propelled and have radios and air-conditioned cabs for the comfort of the driver. The grain goes from these combines directly to a truck that is driven alongside it. Nobody has to tie sacks or load them onto a wagon—talk about having it made!

John Brantley always kept his machinery in good working order and down-time was not very often. One day, a piece of chain on the combine broke and everything stopped. Having to stop combining in the middle of the field was more aggravating than a loose hoe handle when you were chopping cotton.

Jimmy Johnson, a friend of mine from Shepherd school, was helping that day and John told us boys we could ride in the bed of the truck to Charlotte with him to get a part for the combine. John was in a hurry to get back to the field before it rained and was driving pretty fast. Jimmy and I were standing in the back of the truck leaning over the cab and taking in the sights of the big city when John turned a corner a little too fast at a busy intersection. Jimmy didn't lean in time and tumbled out of the truck right into the middle of the street. An ambulance was directly behind us and the medics came running when they saw what happened. Well, Jimmy just jumped up and climbed back into the truck bed and beat on the cab roof to let John know that he was fine and to get the show on the road. We all got back without further incident, John got the combine running again in no time, and we finished the job before it rained.

Every time we combined grain, we would invariably scare rabbits out of the field. Once in a while, we would see a baby rabbit; and take off after it. We usually could catch the poor little thing after he tired out. We would play with the baby for a while and then let him go and find his mama.

We would often find these strange vines growing across the ground that had big green bulbs all over them. We called them "Molly-Pops", (some people called them May-Pops), because they made a popping sound when we stomped on them. I had no idea what they really were or if they had any use—except for us country kid's entertainment. Now I know those wonderful plants are really known as Passion Flowers. You could see us all over the field, stomping and laughing as we popped the bulbs. It was a game to see who could make theirs pop the loudest.

Between chasing rabbits and stomping "Molly-Pops", we would eventually get the wagon loaded and take it to the barn, corn crib, or granary and unload the grain. It was extremely hot in the little space over the milking parlor where we had to unload the barley. I was the smallest of the Ketchie kids, so they would throw me up there to empty the sacks. The dust and chaff from the grain would make me itch something terrible. There wasn't much room left after the grain was poured into the bins and I really had trouble getting my breath. I would invariably have an asthma attack just about every time we unloaded grain into any of those suffocating storage areas. The grain had to be stirred by hand from time to time to keep it from souring or getting too hot. There was always the possibility of the grain catching fire from internal combustion. (I ain't making this stuff up!) It really would catch fire if we didn't keep it stirred. That was another job that I could do without any help.

Mooresville Flour Mills was located on Main Street and all the local farmers would bring their wheat crop to town to sell it to the mill. Sometimes, we would have to get in line as far north on Main Street as McNeely Avenue. The line of wagons would reach as far as I could see. Taking the wheat to town was fun! We didn't have to do any thing but lie on the sacks and pull the wagon forward when our time came. When we got down to *The First and Last Chance* on the corner of Statesville Avenue and Main Street, we would jump off, run in, and get us a pack of nabs and an RC. *The First and Last Chance* was an old time general store shaded by a huge willow oak tree. At one time, it was the first chance you had to buy something as you came into Mooresville and the last chance to buy something as you were leaving.

We would eventually make our way down Main Street until we finally reached the mill. We would untie the sacks of wheat and pour the contents into a grate that led to some scales. The wheat would then be weighed; Uncle Gordon would get his check for the wheat, and usually a hundred pound sack of flour as part of his pay. Aunt Lib did a lot of baking so the flour didn't last as long as you would think. Just as long as she made those sugar cookies, I was all right.

One time, Uncle Tom Brantley was combining wheat for Uncle Otis Honeycutt and Roger, Daddy, and I went to help. Uncle Otis had hired Roger to tie sacks and my first cousin, Danny Wilhelm, and I were to load the wagon. Daddy was visiting with Uncle Otis and not paying too much attention to what was going on with us two boys. Danny was a big boy for his age and always picked on me. He liked to stretch the truth sometime to make a big impression and this time, Danny was bragging about how strong he was.

Well, I had about all the bragging I could take for one day. I told him to back up to the wagon so I could roll a big sack of wheat onto his back. I challenged him and said, "See if you can carry this hundred-and-twenty-pound sack of wheat to the other side of the field."

Uncle Otis and Daddy overheard the exchange between us two boys and started watching with interest as the challenge was picked up by Danny. They didn't say a word but they were holding back their laughter. I rolled that huge sack of wheat onto Danny's back and it didn't even faze the boy one bit, so I climbed on top of the sack. That scoundrel carried me <u>and</u> the hundred-and-twenty-pound sack of wheat all the way across the field and never even breathed hard. Daddy and Uncle Otis got a big kick out of that display of brute strength. I think that Danny and I were only about eleven or twelve years old at the time and he was already as strong as an ox.

Harvesting field corn was a job that had to be done in the late fall. Uncle Gordon had a big field of corn below Aunt Sarah's house on Rinehardt Road. We would have to drive the horses and wagon through the woods and across Uncle Frank Ketchie's lane to get to Aunt Sarah's. The wagon ride itself was fun.

The wagon was fitted with big side-boards and driven between the rows of corn. We had already picked the ears off the stalks by hand and placed them in neat piles. I got to drive the wagon and stop at the piles of corn. Everyone else threw the corn into the wagon. When we had loaded all the corn, we began our journey home. An adult would drive the horses on Rinehardt Road until we reached Uncle Frank's property. It was safer going through the woods and lanes, so I would get to drive the team all the way to Grandma's corncrib. We unloaded the dried field corn into the crib where it was kept until needed.

Some of that field corn was left for seed and some was shelled for the horses. We had a corn-sheller mounted on a wooden box at the corn crib. Joe and I were often relegated to the job of shelling corn. We would stuff an ear of the hard corn down into the sheller and crank like crazy until the cob would shoot out the back. Shelling corn wasn't necessarily a punishment for something that we had done. I tend to think of it as a temporary diversion—it didn't eliminate the mischief we were probably going to get into—it just postponed it, that's all.

When we finished shelling, we would take a load of corncobs and put them in a box behind the wood-stove in the kitchen. Grandma would take some of the cobs from the box and place them in an old kerosene-filled coffee can that she kept on the shelf over the stove. She used the kerosene-soaked cobs to start the fire in the stove every morning. Nothing went to waste at Grandma's house.

I only remember participating in one corn shucking and it was held in front of Uncle Frank's barn one late fall evening. He had a gigantic pile of corn waiting for us when we got there. It looked like it was over seven or eight feet high. You would have thought it impossible for us to have shucked every ear of corn in that huge pile. But, there were a lot of us shuckers participating and we had lots of fun, talking and joking with one another as we worked. Every ear of Uncle Frank's corn was shucked before the night was over.

There was a black family that lived in a house on Uncle Frank's property that did the cooking for all of us that evening. We ate at their house and the food was really delicious. They must have heard that I was going to be there, because they had a large variety of pies and cakes. The entire evening is still a pleasant memory.

I wish young people today could have the opportunity to participate in a good corn shucking and drive a team of horses. Loading a few sacks of grain on a wagon wouldn't hurt them either.

# Filling Silos

Not much happened in the summertime that was more memorable than filling silos around our neighborhood farms. This was an annual event that I greatly anticipated. All the neighbors that had small farms like we did depended on each other to get the job done. It was a serious and monumental task, but it was carried out with much enjoyment.

Some of the farmers that participated included Uncle Gordon, John Brantley, Clarence Brotherton Jay and Bill Neill, Vance Sherrill, Robert Oliphant, and Jimmy Neel Sometimes the Cornelius twins, Homer and Henry, also joined in the group of farmers that took advantage of the help that neighbors extended to each other.

John Brantley was my Daddy's first cousin and had the biggest farm. He was also the one who had the major equipment needed to make silo filling possible. John only had a single-row, corn cutter in the early '50's. Some hired laborers would take corn knives and cut a few rows by hand so that the corn cutter and tractor would have room to get into the field. John would begin the hundreds of trips around and around the field, painstakingly cutting the corn with the cutter. This machine would cut the corn stalks near the ground. The stalks would then have to be loaded, by hand, onto wagons. It was a hot and itchy job. I was glad that I was just a little boy and only had to drive the tractor that pulled the wagon.

The loaded wagon would then be brought to the silo where it was backed up to the chopper-blower. The corn would be unloaded by hand and fed into the machine that chopped it into small pieces and sent it up a huge pipe to the top of the silo. John Brantley's brother, Paul, was in charge of this step.

In the early '50's, Uncle Gordon only had temporary silos that were made of wire and heavy black paper. They would start erecting the thing one layer at a time and blow the silage into it. They built them just twelve to fifteen feet high. Only two or three of the silos were needed for Grandma's small farm.

A few years later, Uncle Gordon hired two black masons, John and Paul Parker, to erect a genuine, brick silo near the barn. That thing was thirty feet tall. Daddy and Uncle Gordon made a wooden ladder and a chute, covered with tin, all the way to the top of the silo. When the silo was filled, the silage would be thrown down the chute to a waiting trailer where it would be taken to the barn to feed the cows. The ladder was the only way to go up or down, and you had to be really careful, or you could fall down the chute and "skin your ignorance". That was what I was told, but I really think they didn't want us to damage their chute.

When I advanced in years to the ripe old age of eleven or twelve, I was promoted to working on the inside of the silo. Uncle Gordon, Charlie Bell Coone, and I were in charge of taking the dangling pipe that was extended down into the silo; and using it to spread the silage evenly. Sometimes that stuff would come out with such force that it was hard to hold on to the pipe. I would have to put it on my shoulder as I aimed it all around the silo. We used our feet to spread it evenly all the way to the edges, and then packed it down by tromping and tromping the stuff as hard as we could. This was summertime, folks. It was hotter than a depot stove inside that silo! We had no fresh air like the outside workers did, but we didn't have the hot sun either; so I guess it evened out. I really think they put me in there to keep me out of the way, but I did help. It was a necessary job, and most everybody else didn't like being inside the silo.

Charlie Bell would light a Camel cigarette, put that thing in his mouth, and never take it out until it almost burned his lip. I always watched to see how long the ashes would grow until they fell off. Sometimes, he would smoke the entire thing, and the ashes would still be hanging on. I still wonder how in the world he did that; I never did understand physics. He would then, simply take his tongue and push the remains of his cigarette out of his mouth.

I guess some unfortunate bovine unknowingly ate what was left of Charlie Bell's cigarette. Uncle Gordon chewed tobacco and I guess he deposited some of that nasty stuff into the silage, too. I wonder if any of Uncle Gordon's cows ever got cancer from all that discarded tobacco.

Well, getting back to work! There were openings every few feet in the side of the silo where the silage could be thrown out and down the chute to an awaiting trailer that was parked beneath it. The trailer would then be rolled to the barn to feed the cows. When the depth of the silage grew deep enough, we would have to insert a door in the opening and lock it from the inside. We then spread silage over it and kept repeating the process until we filled the entire silo. It was always a big thrill when we topped out. You could finally see the world outside again—and from a lofty perch. The next trick was to get down. Grandma's silo didn't have a top on it and we had to be extremely careful when we were at the very last level or we would fall thirty feet to the ground. We would have to crawl over the edge to the wooden ladder that went down the tin-covered chute and carefully descend to the bottom.

John Brantley and the Cornelius twins owned huge silos that had little metal ladders that ran down the outside. Their silos were anywhere from forty to sixty feet tall. We were always extra careful when we had to emerge from the little hole in the top of the metal-domed roofs of one of their silos. I remember carefully climbing down the narrow ladders on the outside of their silos in the fresh air all the way to the ground. It was a little scary for this pre-adolescent. (That is just another way of saying that I was not a teenager yet and I could still be tolerated.) I never gave it much thought, but I might have already been a pain in the neck, and that was the reason I was exiled to the inside of the silo.

**My painting of the Cornelius barn and silo**

I will always remember one particular time while filling the silo at Vance Sherrill's farm. I always had to eat at the table with the rest of the boys and the black laborers. This was called "second table". I didn't mind; there was always plenty of good food. While the older men were lying around outside in the shade, rubbing their bellies, we would be inside, filling ours at the table. When we were ready to start back to work, Miss Cornea, Vance Sherrill's sister, come flying out of the house, asking who had been chewing bubble gum. I had been, but didn't know why that would upset her. There may have been a law about chewing bubble gum while filling a silo—I didn't know. Come to find out, she was having some fun at my expense in front of the older guys. She was cleaning the table and came to my plate, but found out she couldn't pick it up. The plate was stuck to the table. She soon discovered my four-piece-bubble-gum-wad stuck to the bottom of it. I had placed it under my plate for safekeeping and was planning on chewing it some more when I got back into the silo. Good gum was hard to come by, and I already had it worked up good, too. I don't know how in the world I had forgotten that bubble-gum. It just wasn't like me to forget anything that involved something sweet. Everybody got a good laugh over my plate sticking to the table and we soon got back to work.

I honestly think that we were fed the best when we were filling our silo at Grandma's house. Well, it wasn't our silo; but you know what I mean. Grandma and Aunt Lib worked awfully hard to have fried chicken, roast beef, country ham, green beans, mashed potatoes, tomatoes, fried okra, lima beans, fresh corn, and just about anything else you could imagine weighing the table down. I did my part in lightening the poor table's load. Aunt Lib made the best strawberry shortcake in the state of North Carolina. She also made the best "swamp-nosed" chocolate pies you have ever put in your mouth. The meringue on top was so thick that, every time you tried to take a big bite, your nose would swamp up in it.

The older men would lie on the corner porch; dangle their feet off the edge, and moan while comparing notes about the sumptuous meal. I had to eat at the second table; and by the time I'd finished my third plate of food and one plate of dessert, it would be about time for us to start to work again. There wasn't time for us to lie around and moan, like the older guys. We all wanted to take a lengthy break before we went back to work, too. Heck, some of us could barely move.

Grandma and Aunt Lib didn't get to eat until all of us were fed. Then, they had the awful job of washing all those dishes and cleaning up the hot kitchen. Filling silos was extremely hard work for everyone involved. I never heard anyone complain—except, maybe yours truly, but I never once complained about the food.

I didn't mind working my scrawny, little butt off for the meals we were fed while filling silos.

Silos didn't have a whole lot to do when they were empty. They would just sit there beckoning us boys to try some foolish things. Once in a while, Roger would climb to the top of Uncle Gordon's thirty-foot tall silo when it was empty and walk a lap around the top of the bricks. He could have fallen either to the inside or the outside, all the way to the bottom. That was entirely his option. Sometimes, I worried about that boy.

**Uncle Gordon's silo**

I was never that daring; I was too much of a "fraidy cat" or "chicken" to do most of the things he attempted. He was a lot more agile than I ever hoped to be. I wasn't exactly clumsy, but I was what you might say "athletically challenged". Daddy always told me, "You ain't nothin' but main strength and orkedness." I had no idea in the world what that was, but he said it an awful lot! Sometime later, I realized it was his way of calling me awkward, and I knew exactly what that meant. I was definitely that.

Summertime memories were many, but few that pertain to work stand out as much as filling silos. They were good times with good friends and good food.

# Hog Killing Day

I can still hear my Daddy now: "Get up! You goin' to stay in bed all day?" Getting me out from under the three heavy quilts, where it was warm and cozy, was not an easy job.

There was no heat in our house, except in the parlor where the little, Warm Morning Stove was doing its level best to replace the numbing cold with the warmth that could come only from a good, wood-fired stove. Of course, I didn't want to move my little tail from my warm cocoon; and predictably, Daddy would grab the covers and yank them completely off the bed with a quick flick of his wrist. He was really good at that! I couldn't lie in bed very long without any covers over me, or I would soon be shivering like a lost puppy. Daddy knew that, too!

Mumbling and complaining, my feet would hit the ice-cold floor, and I would hurry to the struggling, little stove where Daddy had lit a fire about 4:30 in the morning. I couldn't imagine anybody getting up at that time of day, but now I get up around 4:00 every day, too. It's funny how age changes things. It never dawned on me that there was no warm fire awaiting Daddy when he got up. I just took that for granted.

I had not given a thought to what the day had in store or why I had been made to get up so early. If I had, I would have already been up and finished eating my mush and sausage by now. After all, it was almost 6:00, and it was "Hog Killing Day". I couldn't wait to get down to Grandma's house and help get the big fire started under the huge cauldron we used to boil gallons and gallons of water. We kids looked forward to this special day each year. Uncle Gordon; Aunt Lib; Cousin Joe; Aunt Ruth; my big brother,

Roger; my sister, Laura; Daddy; a few neighbors; and I would show up for this momentous occasion. Sometimes Aunt Sarah, a few of her children, and Aunt Catherine would be there, too. It was a neighborhood event.

We always had two or three hogs of our own that were fattened up on acorns that we picked up from all over our backyard—one little bucket at a time. We fed our hogs barrels of acorns. They loved them and ate those things like a bunch of hogs, too! Daddy raised black and white Poland China and the red-colored Tamworth hogs. I couldn't tell the difference when they were fried into sausage patties. A hog was a hog to me.

Uncle Gordon and Grandma raised the big Poland China hogs and they were kept in a lot behind their barn. Since all the hog killing was going on at Grandma's; we usually killed theirs first, and then ours would be next. I thought that was pretty fair.

Daddy would shoot the selected hogs between their eyes with his trusty, Remington pump .22, rifle. When it was agreed that the animals were good and dead, one of the adults would slit their throats to bleed them out before the hogs were loaded on a trailer for transport. Then, they were hauled to the ancient oak tree beside the granary. It provided a convenient limb for the block and tackle that was used to hoist the huge hogs into the scalding water. The older folks would carry the dangerously hot water from the cauldron in five-gallon buckets and carefully pour it into the waiting fifty-five-gallon barrel that was situated right under the block and tackle. Uncle Gordon would take his index finger and rake it through the water. Roger explained to me that he was testing the water to see if it was the right temperature. Uncle Gordon did that three times, and if it burned his finger by the third swipe, the water was too hot. If the water was not the right temperature, the hog's hair would be really difficult to scrape off the hide.

When Uncle Gordon was satisfied with the temperature of the water, it was time to lift one of the huge, unfortunate, porcine corpse; by the hind legs with the block and tackle. It was lifted high enough to let the entire thing down, headfirst, into the scalding water. That would be done about three times. Either Uncle Gordon or Daddy would take a huge, sharp knife and slit the great, white belly open so that the intestines and organs could be removed and dropped into a big, tin tub. Most of us young kids would find somewhere else to be when this was going on because the smell was sickening. The liver and other organs were used in the making of livermush and souse meat. The head was severed and set on a big board so that the hair could be scraped off and the brains removed. Grandma immediately took the brains, went to the house, and scrambled them with eggs for her breakfast. She said she liked brains and eggs. Why, I don't know. Mother always said, "We ate every part of the hog but the squeal." I believe that was true!

After the head was removed, the carcass was split in half by a sharp ax, wielded by Daddy or Uncle Gordon. These halves were dragged up onto some big boards that were kept just for this purpose. Here, the hair was scraped off with a corn knife until the hide was clean. They made me scrape the hair off the head, snout, and ears with an old, zinc jar lid. They told me it worked better. I don't think they wanted me to have a big knife like they used. All of us helped scrape. Most of the head would be cut up to go into the livermush. Daddy's sister, my Aunt Catherine, usually took the tub of intestines and meticulously removed all the fat from them that she possibly could. This fat would be added to more fat as the hog was cut into pieces.

That night, Grandma and Aunt Lib cooked up a big supper of fresh tenderloin, and dozens of Aunt Lib's homemade biscuits that were baked in the old wood-stove. It was a feast—to say the least. And some people wonder why I liked killing hogs.

The next morning greeted us with more work—but also more fun. We would rise early and build fires under a couple

137

more black pots. These were smaller than the huge cauldron used for boiling water. These were for the good stuff! All the fat was dumped into one of the pots and the stirring began. The fire rendered the grease from the fat until we ended up with a huge pot of the hot liquid. Chunks of the cooked fat would be left floating near the surface, to be scooped up with a big, long-handled ladle. These pieces would then be deposited into the lard press where I had the job of turning the handle that squeezed the last bit of grease out of the chunks of fat. The hot liquid was strained through a piece of cloth that hung under the press into a five-gallon, lard can. I would crank the press back up and open it to the sweet smell of hot cracklings. We would dump them into a big dishpan and immediately seize the tasty morsels and start eating. I really liked them steaming hot and fresh out of the press. The rest would be taken inside the house, and Aunt Lib would add pieces of the cracklings to her cornbread.

The retired liver mush pot

Daddy could be found standing over the other big, black pot, stirring and seasoning the livermush. He used a huge wooden paddle that Uncle Gordon made just for this purpose. I think Daddy and Uncle Gordon were the only ones that knew all the secret ingredients that went into this tasty stuff. When they were satisfied that it was done, it was dipped out and ladled into large dishpans where it would cool and harden. We sold a lot of our livermush to McLean's Supermarket and City Grocery and Market in downtown Mooresville. City folks just ate it up. We had quite a good reputation for making some of the best livermush in the area—if I do have to say so myself.

The entire hog had to be cut into pieces. Some of the shoulders and other tasty cuts were used for making sausage. Sometimes we took the meat downtown to City Grocery and Market and let John McLean grind it up for us. That was so much easier and faster than using our old, hand-cranked, sausage grinder. We brought the ground-up meat back to Grandma's and put it into pans where Daddy started seasoning it and mixing it up with his hands. There was a secret recipe that he used for making sausage, too. I know Daddy liked to add a lot of sage to ours.

The next day, even more work was waiting for Daddy and Uncle Gordon. Other adults would join in and help them rub down the hams, the remaining shoulders, and the side meat with special ingredients only they knew. I remember it took a lot of salt. Some hams were sugar-cured and some were salt-cured. They were then hung in the smokehouse where hickory wood slowly smoked the meat until the savory fragrance permeated it all. They were left to hang in the cool smokehouse until they were properly aged. The side meat and fat back were also taken into the smokehouse and put on shelves. Some country hams and side meat were later sold to restaurants and grocery stores in town. We needed the money and didn't keep many hams for our own use.

The side meat (or "Streak of Lean" as we called it) was fried for breakfast and used for seasoning green beans and other good stuff. It was almost impossible to scrape all the hair off the side meat and invariably some hair would show up on the rind.

I will always remember the time Uncle Otis and Aunt Marie Honeycutt took Mother and me to Richmond, Virginia to see Daddy when he was in the Veteran's Hospital. I had never eaten any kind of bought-meat before, and when Uncle Otis ordered our breakfast of bacon and eggs, I noticed the bacon looked a lot different from what we had at home. He asked me if everything was all right with my food because I kept looking at the bacon. I told him the bacon didn't have any hair on it. He laughed and assured me that it was fit for human consumption. I still remember, to this day, the taste of that piece of bacon. I think it was the sweetest bacon I ever put in my mouth.

**Checking on our future bacon with Daddy**

I also remember frying strips of "Streak of Lean" and eating all the meat, except the rind. We liked to save the rinds for later, just to have something to chew on as a snack.

Laura, especially, liked it and would wrap some pieces of the leftover rind in some waxed paper and carry it in the back pocket of her blue jeans for emergencies. One day, we were teasing Grandma's big dog named "Mac". Laura would make him run to the length of his chain and laugh when he couldn't catch her, but that day, he smelled those pork rinds in her back pocket and would not be denied the tasty snack. He knocked Laura down and started chewing on her back pocket until she gave up the pork rinds.

It is hard to explain just how much work went into the everyday life of small farm families such as ours. Grandma's farm was so close to our home that we were involved with everything that went on there just like it was our own. In a sense, I suppose it was. Killing hogs may sound brutal to some folks, but it was a necessary thing to do if we wanted any meat for the rest of the year. We ate just about anything that wouldn't eat us! I would not have had it any other way.

# Possum Hunting

A possum is a nocturnal marsupial that dwelled in the woods around where we lived. A possum really looks like a big ugly rat and weighs about seven or eight pounds. I heard that some people actually called these ugly, little beasts, opossums. I just couldn't bring myself to do that. What would it sound like to my friends if I said, "I think we are going opossum hunting tonight? Would you care to go?" We just said, "We're goin' possum huntin'. Y'onta go?" What do you truthfully think sounds natural?

We loved possum hunting in the fall and winter months. Robert Oliphant's woods had a lot of possums and coons, too. (That's raccoons to city folks.) His woods were located directly across from our house. All you had to do was walk through Mr. Sink's field, go through Aunt Lil Patten's woods, cross a couple more fields, some more woods, then jump a stream or two and his woods were right there. Just like I said—his woods were directly across from our house.

Late fall was the best time to go. Robert's sweet potato crop would have just been harvested, and there would always be a few sweet potatoes left scattered across the ground. We would take our pocketknives, peel those suckers and eat them raw, as we picked them up, right off the ground. They were a real treat, and if we didn't catch a possum, we at least had some good "sweet taters". Often, when we didn't get a possum, we would load our sack with all we could carry of the tasty treasures.

The Oliphants were known for raising lots of produce, so Daddy called them truck farmers. I never quite understood that terminology. They never raised trucks—they raised produce for gosh sakes! Anyway, the reason I brought that up was because they also raised a bunch of turnips, greens and pumpkins in the fall along with sweet potatoes. Almost every time we went hunting on their place, we got to eat. Eating was always important to me. Those raw turnips were mighty good to chew on while climbing all over the countryside, listening to the dogs and looking for a frightened possum to kidnap.

Sometimes it would be so cold that we had to build a fire to keep us warm while we listened for the dogs to tree a possum or a coon. A coon is a striped-tailed critter that wears a mask, washes his food in the branch, climbs trees, and will fight your possum dogs in the blink of an eye. They were often called raccoons by people who were not from around here. I actually heard somebody call them that one time, but they weren't related to me.

One winter night, Donald West joined us for the fun. I don't think he was very used to being outside at night in the cold winter air. Daddy wasn't with us; so we got to build a little fire. The dogs had lost the possum scent and started chasing a fox. That just meant that we were going to have to wait a long while for them to come back. It was so cold, Donald's teeth started chattering and he said he couldn't stand it anymore. He took our lantern and poured the kerosene out of it onto the fire, and it made a pretty substantial blaze. He abruptly climbed right up on that fire and just stood there. All was well for a while. Then, all of a sudden, Donald started yelling and jumping around like something serious was wrong with the boy. He fell to the ground, hollering; and took off his shoes as quickly as he could get the things unlaced. The soles of his shoes were bubbling! I guess some of the heat from that blaze had worked its way through the soles and all the way to his feet. Roger and I didn't try that stunt—being the astute young men that we were. Seeing Don lying on the cold ground, writhing in pain made a lasting impression on us.

The dogs got further and further away, chasing that blasted fox. It got colder and colder as time wore on, and we finally gave up on the dogs and went home to get warm. The dogs came straggling in about five o'clock the next morning, looking tired and worn out.

Another night in particular comes to mind. It was a cold night and we were possum hunting in Robert Oliphant's woods. There was a huge tree standing beside a steep bank that ran along the branch. The dogs were having fits, barking wildly and trying to climb the tree. We shined our lights up among the branches, trying to find whatever the dogs had treed. David Wilson vowed that he could definitely climb that tree and declared that he should be the one to do it. We didn't argue with him—he had his heart set on it. That big, old hickory looked like it was the tallest tree in the whole danged woods. I didn't know why the possum had to pick that particular tree, but I guess he knew what he was doing.

We got our hands together and gave David a boost so that he could get hold of the bottom limb. He started climbing higher and higher while we were shining our lights up in there amongst the limbs to try to sight the possum. We were calling to each other to find out if anyone had spotted anything when, all of a sudden, Roger disappeared. We shined our lights all around the base of that tree, but there was no Roger to be found. We faintly heard someone call out for help. The plea sounded far away, but we couldn't figure out from where. Finally, Roger came crawling up from the creek bank. While he was circling and shining his light and looking up into the top of the tree, he backed off the bank and fell all the way down to the creek. He wasn't looking so hot when he joined us. He was wet, muddy, cold and looked a little confused. The rest of us got a good laugh out of his ordeal.

Well, David finally climbed out on a limb and shook a big disgruntled possum out. The unhappy creature landed on the ground with a loud thump and the dogs caught him for us so we could put him in a sack.

We were possum hunting behind Shepherd School one night and were having a great time. The dogs treed one right off the bat and our chief tree climber, David Wilson, shimmied up the tree and shook a great big possum out so the dogs could catch him. We wrestled it away from the dogs, and were ready to put him in the sack, only to find that we had forgotten to bring one. Roger, always the inventive one, suggested that we cut a branch and let the possum just hang by its tail from it, like they do in the trees. Roger held the stick while David put the possum on it. It seemed like the stick trick might work. It did, too, for a while, until that possum climbed up onto the stick and headed straight for Roger's finger. Roger quickly switched ends of the stick, but the possum kept coming toward his hand each time he switched ends. This went on for several end-switches until the possum was a little quicker and finally got himself a good bite of Roger's finger. We didn't hunt too much longer that night. Daddy told us that we should have split the stick and put the possum's tail through it. Of course, he told us this after we got home.

One time we were hunting and catching possums so quickly we didn't know what to do with all of them. We only had two sacks and that was usually enough. We rarely caught over two possums in a single night and we liked to have a sack for each one. (At least we remembered the sacks this time.) The problem was that we caught seven possums. They decided to double up on the population of possums per sack. I didn't think there would be a major problem or anything; I figured that all possums were related and would get along just fine. That's not exactly what happened to the group I was carrying in my sack. I always carried the sack over my shoulder because it was easier, and a sack full of possums got heavy after a while. The possums must have been having a family feud or something, because before I knew what was going on, there was an awful noise coming from the sack on my back. Those nasty things started fighting, and one of them must have gotten whipped up on pretty good. The most awful smell started creeping out from behind me, and the sack started to feel wet on my back. Pretty soon, I was not allowed to accompany my fellow possum hunters. They informed me that the smell that was all over the back of my coat was just more than they could handle—so much for friendship. Evidently possum "pucky" is not a desirable aroma that wins friends and influences people.

We never ate the possums ourselves, but would take them to the west end of town where we would sell them for two dollars apiece. That was good money for just having fun.

I don't suppose that any young people possum hunt any more around this neck of the woods. I never hear the dogs baying off in the distance. I do see a lot more possums now than I used to see when I was young—it's just that they are always lying in the middle of the road. I don't think possums will ever figure out the art of road-crossing.

I still remember with great fondness what it sounded like when our old possum dogs, Drum and Queen, threw their heads back and looked up into a big, old tree and did their wild, enthusiastic barking. It was hard to hold them back after they had treed one. It didn't get a whole lot better than that.

# Snow, Snow, and More Snow

I don't know what it is about a good snow that makes everyone react a little differently. Take us kids for instance; if we knew that it was going to snow, our parents could hardly get us to go to bed. We couldn't wait for daylight so we could go outside and play in it. Some people thought of snow as a troublesome event that had to be endured.

It seemed to me that it snowed more at night than it did in the daytime. I always wondered about that. We would go to the back door and turn on the outside light, hoping to see the first, tiny flakes of snow. It always came from the northwest—or just seemed like it did. Of course, each of us would run back inside and let it be known that "we" were the one to have actually seen the first flake. I had a keen eye and often held that prestigious honor. Now, as I look back on it, maybe I was the only one watching for it anyway. It was real important to me. We would listen to the weatherman everyday and hope for a big snowstorm of at least six inches—then we would get out of school.

One evening, I was eating supper at Grandma's house when she looked out of the dining room window at the giant oak tree beside the granary and, without any more thought, proclaimed, "We're going to have a big snow tonight."

I was quick to tell her, "Grandma, the weatherman is not calling for any snow at all." Clyde (Cloudy) McLean was the authority in our area. He forecasted the weather each day on WBTV, Channel 3, out of Charlotte; and I had just seen him a few minutes before, on Aunt Ruth's television. I looked out the window as the sun disappeared behind the pasture woods, giving the sky a beautiful orange glow. There were a few wispy clouds, but definitely no sign of snow.

Grandma said, "Look at those guineas up in that tree. See how low they are roosting and the way they have pointed themselves. It's going to snow for sure." Well, let me tell you; the next morning we were playing on six inches of the wonderful white stuff. Grandma and Daddy were both really good at predicting the weather. Why did we need Cloudy McLean anyway?

**My painting: "Grandma's Granary"**

I don't know who came up with the tradition of running barefoot in the snow. We were told that if we ran all the way around the house barefoot in it, we wouldn't have any colds that winter. Being the trusting, little boy I was at the time, I was eager to give it a shot. Let me tell you right here and now—snow is cold on bare feet! Laura and I would make our run and fly back into the house, jumping up and down on our frozen feet. Then, we would lie on the floor and hold them next to the stove. They would sting and burn and feel like they were on fire. Mama would wrap warm towels around our feet, and that would help ease the burning sensation. I really believe that is where the term, "the agony of de feet" came from.

Roger decided to run all the way to Grandma's and back, barefoot in the snow. We tried to talk him out of it, but he being older and wiser than we, did it anyway. After that memorable night, I doubted his ability to make sound judgments. I felt better just knowing that his feet froze too.

A layer of sleet on top of the snow would make that crazy ritual even more miserable for us. The icy crust would cut our feet and have them bleeding by the time we made it all the way around the house. It was just another thing we did when it snowed. It might have been a law—I don't know.

Joe or Uncle Gordon would come to our house with the tractor and scrape a path to the calf stable, hog pen, and chicken house for us, so we could feed the animals. They would also scrape the driveway that we shared with Mrs. Blackwelder. While they were there, they would scrape Mr. Malcolm's driveway too. He wasn't likely to be going anywhere, but they did it for him anyway. That's just what neighbors did; they helped each other out as much as they could.

**Laura and Joe scraping the driveway**

We burned coal when we had the $16 to buy a ton of it, but we usually had to burn wood in our little, Warm Morning Stove that was in the parlor. It was our only source of heat. Our next door neighbor, Mr. Malcolm, burned coal all winter. His coal smoke would invariably coat our beautiful, pristine white snow, soon after it fell, with a dirty, blackish-gray film.

We would traipse outside and scoop off the top layer of the dirty snow, dip down into the wonderful, pure white stuff, and fill up a big pot with it, all the way to the brim. This pure snow would be spooned into glasses for each of us. Mama would then mix up a batch of milk, vanilla flavoring and sugar and stir some of that wonderful, sweet liquid into each glass. We all had instant snow cream. That was always one of the first things we did when it snowed because, as soon as it got daylight, we would track it all up, and it wouldn't be fit to use. Snow cream was a fantastic treat that we always looked forward to with great anticipation. It was almost like having free ice cream.

Tracking rabbits in the fresh snow was always a fun sport. Daddy was really good at spotting one sitting under an evergreen branch or among the weeds quicker than I could say "Jack Rabbit." All of us kids would try to sneak up on the unsuspecting prey with practiced stealth and pounce on it before it would take off running. If one did jump and run, we would chase it as fast as we could go, but it had the advantage. The rabbits knew where they were going and would zig and zag through the snow faster than we could. We had a severe zig and zag deficiency, but once in a while, we would run one down and catch it with our bare hands. Usually, the poor thing would be so tired it would just give up. We ate lots of rabbits and squirrels in the winter

**Daddy and Mama tracking rabbits**

Daddy had about a dozen rabbit hollows set all around Uncle Frank's pasture and woods. This added a lot of free meat to our table. I checked the rabbit hollows often for Daddy because he told me to and I didn't have a whole lot of choice in the matter. I was always hoping they would be empty when I looked because I was afraid to reach inside the hollow and pull the poor rabbit out.

One cold morning that stands out in my memory was when I found a hollow with the door that had been tripped. I was really young then—maybe eight or nine years old—and was afraid to open the door by myself. I stuck my finger down the hole that was drilled in the top for the trigger mechanism and felt some warm fur. Well, I was not about to run my hand down in that rabbit box and pull that creature out with my bare hands and give it a good whack behind the head. I ran back to the house and got Roger to come and check it out. He felt sorry for me, and we tracked back into Uncle Frank's woods together. We found the hollow just as I had left it. He promptly stood the box on its rear end so he could open the door, lift the rabbit out, and provide the deathblow. When Roger opened the door and looked in, he jumped back with a funny look on his face. I peered around him to see a great big, possum staring back at us with what looked like a stupid grin on its face. The actual truth is that thing could have bitten my finger off when I stuck it through the hole. Thanks to God again for delivering me from getting hurt because of my ignorance.

Our family depended on rabbits for fresh meat in the winter, so Daddy continued setting his hollows even after all of us kids were grown. He had set sixteen rabbit hollows one year and was looking forward to a successful season. One morning he found that all of his hollows had been chopped to pieces with an ax and tossed in a huge pile. Daddy was devastated at first; but went to his shop and faithfully made sixteen more and set them all back where the others had been destroyed.

A few days later, he discovered that the dastardly deed had been carried out again. All of his hard work was destroyed for the second time. I have mentioned it before; but find it worth repeating: Daddy was a man of faith!

He went back into his shop, prayerfully made sixteen more rabbit hollows and carried each one back to their appropriate places. This time, he took some liquid shoe polish and wrote on each one in big letters; "God is looking".

Daddy never had any more problems with his rabbit hollows as long as he lived.

Usually, we weren't as interested in building snowmen as we were in heading for the pasture behind Grandma's house to go sledding. We had an old, Royster Fertilizer sign that had been bent up in the front to make a terrific sled. Roger said that he thought it might have been a Red Goose Shoes sign, but I'm almost positive it was Royster Fertilizer. Anyway, it was one of those old, porcelain signs that were popular in the '40's and '50's. That sign was as slick as glass on the surface and would fly down the hills. We finally abused the sign so much that it was coming apart where we kept bending it up in front. We were faced with the dilemma of locating some other means of transportation so that we could continue to fly down the ice-covered, pasture hills.

We later found a discarded, '41 Chevrolet car-hood that was even better than the sign. Five or six of us would pile on that thing at the same time and race down the slopes. Crashing was expected and a big part of the fun. We eventually tore the car hood in half and made two sleds out of it. We now had in our possession two of the fastest modes of transportation suitable for the sleet-covered snow. They were so dangerously fast and impossible to stop that we had to bail out before we got near the creek; so we ended up sliding down the hill on our rear ends.

In 1960, it snowed every Wednesday in the month of March, and we had over twenty-one inches of the white stuff on the ground at one time. It would snow about six inches, then sleet a couple of inches on top of that. The accumulation of snow and sleet was so heavy; I being the youngest and the lightest of weight; was asked to climb up on the barn roof and shovel some of it off. The barn was in danger of collapsing from the sheer weight. The sleet on the snow was so thick that even the cows couldn't break through the crust. One of Uncle Gordon's cows fell on the treacherous, icy stuff and broke her leg. Even though she was just an old milk cow, we ate a lot of beef that winter.

I remember going all the way behind Aunt Sarah's house to sled in Mr. Les Blackwelder's pasture. There was a hill so steep that we would have to hold on to a barbed wire fence as we made our way across the top of it. If we didn't, we would start sliding without a sled. Sometimes I would let go of the fence and ski down the icy hill using my shoes as skis.

Once, when Mama went sledding behind Aunt Sarah's with us, we put her on a gentler and more forgiving slope so it wouldn't scare the "stuffing" out of her. There was a huge briar patch that surrounded Mr. Will Blackwelder's old, deserted house, and this was pretty near where the "kind and gentle slope" was located. We often thought Mama to be a "fraidy cat" or a "chicken." When she was ready, we gave her a little nudge, and she started off really well, heading toward Will's deserted house, but she couldn't control her path like we did—her being a rookie and all. Instead she headed straight for the huge briar patch, and we began yelling for her to stop. Those pieces of tin didn't come equipped with brakes and she didn't bail out like we usually did; so she went directly into the thickest part of those briars. We were so afraid she was hurt or, even worse, <u>mad</u>! We ran as fast as we could on the slick ice to find her still on the sled. We thought she was crying but found to our relief; that she was laughing hysterically. We had dodged another bullet!

School was called off for so long that month that the School Board felt guilty and decided that we had to go back to class, even though the ground was still covered with snow and ice. Daddy made me go to school, while he and his friends went sledding. He liked to have fun as much as the next guy. I didn't think it was fair myself.

We talked Uncle Gordon into getting on our half-car-hood sled one time, and he was doing really well at first. I think he was enjoying his ride until it turned around backwards as he reached the bottom of the hill. The back end of that sled dug into the sleet covered snow and just stopped abruptly. Well, Uncle Gordon kept on going, and the back of his head hit the thick crust of ice so hard it made a big hole in it with an awful thud. He got up, unceremoniously picked up his cap, put it crookedly on his head, and carefully walked back to Grandma's. He never said a word, and neither did we. We did go back and look at the spot where he hit the ice, and there was a hole just the size of Uncle Gordon's head. We never told him about that either.

We never had the fancy, down-filled parkas and fur-lined gloves like everyone has today. Those nylon snowsuits that skiers use are just too good to be true. (We didn't have them either.) We wore our blue jeans—sometimes with insulated underwear beneath them. We had thin, cotton gloves or some inexpensive leather ones that got wet immediately and made the cold, wet snow hurt our hands even more. I remember playing outside in the beautiful snow and sometimes crying at the same time because I was so miserably cold and wet. We would sweep the snow off our feet at the back door and undress by the Warm Morning Stove in the parlor. Clothes would be hanging all over the room. I would hang my wet clothes as near the stove as possible, to get them dry in a hurry so I could go back outside and get to be miserable all over again.

**Roger and me in our snow attire**

There are many more fond memories of playing in the snow. These are just a few of them.

# Country Stores

Country stores have always been popular places for young boys and old men to hang out. That is where we boys got most of our formal education about some of the mysteries of life. Some of that education could not have been obtained anywhere else.

Carl Harkey's store had an old, pot-bellied stove that reigned in the midst of a huge box of sand. The sand had the responsibility of catching ashes from the stove and soaking up the tobacco juice that was projected its way by the serious checker players.

Checkers was the main attraction at Carl's store. We played on a homemade checkerboard, using old discarded bottle caps for checkers. One player would have his caps turned upside down, and his opponent would have his turned right side up, showing the name-brands of the soft drinks. Up North, they call soft drinks "sodas" or "pop". Don't you just hate that? I don't ever remember asking for a bottle of "pop" in my life. I would have been embarrassed to death.

A lot of soft drinks were consumed at the local store while the conversations droned on and on and the checker playing intensified. Most drinks were accompanied by a "Moon Pie", or a pack of "Nabs" (cheese crackers). It was almost a tradition to pour a pack of Lance peanuts into your Co-Coler, (that's Southern for Cocoa-Cola) and swish them around a little bit before taking a big taste of the freshly created delicacy. This was an added treat, but it cost a nickel more for the luxury. I usually couldn't afford that, but it all depended on how many empty bottles I could pick up from the roadside on my way to the store. At three cents apiece, it mounted up. Some people would throw empty bottles out of their car windows like it was the acceptable thing to do. That was something that I never did. I was taught to take pride in our beautiful countryside and my daddy would have "cleaned my clock" if he knew that I had ever thrown trash out of a car window. I am disappointed that litter is so prevalent along our highways, today.

My next door neighbor, Mr. June Blackwelder, taught me how to play a competent game of Checkers, and sometimes I could hold my own with the guys at the store. David Wilson was one of the better checker players, and I enjoyed beating him more than anybody. The reason being— he hated to lose worse than anyone else. I remember beating my daddy twenty-one straight games of Checkers. He wouldn't play me any more. David still would; he just couldn't stand the thought that a little boy could beat him. David and I played even after I got married and became pretty evenly matched in our Checker playing abilities.

Rook and Set Back were two of the more popular card games that were played at Carl Harkey's store. I learned to play Rook rather capably and the older fellows would let me sit in on their games. I really got excited when the Rook card was dealt to me. I knew I could bid more; or either turn a trick with it against an opponent. Seeing the picture of that old crow on the Rook card always gave me a thrill because I knew that I held the most powerful card in the deck. Some folks play the entire game of Rook without the Rook card, but I don't think it is nearly as exciting.

I remember one night at our house; Daddy and I were playing against Roger and David Wilson in a hotly contested, Rook marathon. Mama made us take our game out to the shop because we were keeping her awake. We were just going to play a few games, but David and Roger kept losing, and David didn't want to quit while they were behind; so we built a big fire in the stove, and the Rook war began. It lasted into the wee hours of the morning, with Roger and David being the big losers. David didn't want to play too much Rook with Daddy and me after that.

Pitching horseshoes was another favorite pastime at the local country stores. We pitched beside Obie Davis' store on Highway 21 and also at Carl Harkey's Oak Grove Filling Station.

One hot, summer day, we were pitching shoes behind Carl's store, and the Japanese hornets were becoming a real nuisance. Those hornets were mean and would sting you in a heartbeat. We were constantly being distracted and couldn't concentrate on our form. We needed to practice so that we not only played well, but looked good doing it. It wasn't that we were professionals or anything; we just didn't want to look like a bunch of rookies—sometimes girls would come and watch us pitch. Those hateful hornets were coming from a white oak tree that was near where we were pitching. David Wilson, being the impetuous one that he was, took about all this hornet business he could stand. He went to the store and pumped about a gallon of regular gas into a bucket—he said he didn't need high-test gas to kill a hornet. Well, he just walked right up to that hornet's nest, threw the bucket of gas on it, and took off running as fast as he could toward the store. David had gone about ten yards when a great big hornet popped him on the back of the elbow with so much force it knocked him down. He tumbled a few more yards, got up, and with more hornets chasing him, ran some more. He finally made it to the safety of the store. Roger pumped some more gas and threw it on the nest after things quieted down, and I think that took care of the hornet problem for the rest of the year. Poor David's arm swelled to about three times its natural size and really looked funny. That is one feat I never saw David attempt again.

We pitched a lot of horseshoes at our house, too, in the summertime. Our next-door neighbor, Mr. June Blackwelder would join us when we were pitching and would often be Daddy's partner. He was quite skillful at the game and a lot of fun. I remember he would start calling me "Whitey", because he knew I didn't like that. He also knew that when I got upset, I couldn't pitch worth a "rat's hat". Upsetting me seemed to be part of his strategy, so he would then call me "George"—I didn't like that, either; and then he would call me "Cotton Top". Well, that really got me upset! Daddy and Mr. Blackwelder would beat Roger and me just about every time Mr. Blackwelder would tease me. Thanks to his constant teasing, I finally accepted the sobriquet of "Cotton". I didn't say I liked it—I said I finally accepted it. I have now been called that descriptive epithet for over fifty years, thanks to "good ol' Mr. Blackwelder". The girls in high school thought it was kind of cute, so I had to get used to it—like it or not.

Horseshoes was my game! It didn't require a whole lot of energy to pitch horseshoes and that was right down my alley. I could hold my own with just about any of the other guys. Daddy and I also pitched a lot of horseshoes against Roger and David. We won our share of games against them, too. I think having Daddy for a partner gave me the decided edge.

One of Carl Harkey's younger brothers, Russell, and I played mumble-peg just about every time I went to Carl's store. We would face each other while straddling an old wooden bench that sat out front in the shade. The bench was ideal for mumble-peg. The game was simple and a lot of fun to play when you had some good competition. Russell and I would play for hours if we were caught up on our chores at home.

The game was played with a two-bladed pocketknife. The big blade was set to point straight out from the knife with the smaller blade set perpendicular to it. Setting it up this way; made the knife resemble the letter "T". The object of the game was to stick the perpendicular blade into the wooden bench; then flip it in the air toward the other fellow. (I realize we were facing each other, but we never flipped the knife all the way into the other person.) If the big blade came down and stuck into the wood with the knife handle sticking straight up, you scored one hundred points. If it landed with the two blades sticking in the wood and the handle was not touching, you earned seventy-five points. If the knife landed with only the perpendicular short blade in the wood and nothing else touching, you scored fifty points. If the short blade stuck, and the handle was touching, all you earned was twenty-five points. If nothing stuck at all and the knife fell over, you scored nothing and lost your turn. As long as you were earning points, you kept on flipping. We usually played until one of us got to five hundred points. It sounds complicated, but it wasn't—or I couldn't have played it. It was a lot of fun for us simple, country boys.

I remember pumping gas for Carl when I was just thirteen or fourteen years old. There was a gas war going on in the 1950's, and during this time, we pumped gas for thirteen cents a gallon. The cars would be lined up, all the way from the pumps, to the highway. We pumped so much one day that we blew four or five fuses—Carl's wiring was not the best in the world. Everybody was anxious to get some of that cheap gas.

While gas was so inexpensive, all of us guys would chip in a quarter each so we could buy enough gas for Roger or David Wilson to ride us around all afternoon.

It was about the time of the great gas war that Carl came up with the idea of giving away fifty gallons of gas every week. Daddy was one of the lucky winners, and our family was able to do a lot of riding around on that free gas. Our old 1950 Plymouth didn't look so hot, but it got fairly good gas mileage.

Bill Overcash's Store was located south of our house toward town. It was a little closer than Carl's store and Mama would often send us kids to pick up something for her when she needed it in a hurry.

I remember the time Roger and I were recruited to go and purchase a box of kitchen matches. We always jumped at the chance to go to the store—sometimes we could get a little candy with any change that was left over. Well, walking along the highway toward home, we started tossing the box of matches to each other as a game. Everything was going really well until Roger threw the box a little too high for me. I, being the clumsy kid I was, made an unsuccessful leap to catch it, but failed. Have you ever seen an entire box of kitchen matches explode before your eyes? I have! That's what happened when that box hit the pavement. The really tough part was going home to face Mama with no matches and no money—we had already eaten up the change.

Overcash's store sold hog feed packaged in one-hundred pound sacks that were made of beautifully printed fabrics. Mama made a lot of my shirts from that free material—free if you bought the hog feed. Those sacks of feed were extremely heavy, and Bill had them piled really high in the back of his store. I invariably would want my shirt to be made from the material of one of the sacks at the bottom of the stack. Bill wasn't about to move thousands of pounds of hog feed so I could get a particular sack. I would have to wait until he sold all of the ones piled on top of it before I could get mine.

When I was in the third or fourth grade, I remember picking out this special sack I wanted so badly. It was a printed scene of a Hawaiian boy and palm trees. My Lord, it was pretty! Bill promised that he would not let anybody else have it.

He was good to his word and informed us when the time had come that we could pick up my prized feed sack. Daddy loaded it in the trunk of the Plymouth and brought it home, emptied the contents in the feed-barrel in the car shed, and gave the coveted material to Mama so she could began sewing my new shirt. She had to wash the material first— that slowed things down considerably.

Mother finally made my shirt out of that beautiful material, and I could hardly wait to wear it to school because I wanted to make a big impression on Lynda Wilhelm, and I was hoping that this new shirt would do the trick.

Lynda was as pretty as a speckled pup under a covered wagon and I was doing my level best to get noticed by this young, brunette beauty. I was planning on strutting around a little bit during recess where she would be sure to see me in my new shirt. I had it all planned out in advance.

Well, Danny Wilhelm, my first cousin, and I got into a disagreement. Danny was a big boy and wasn't scared of "doodley squat". We ended up in a schoolboy scuffle, and Danny grabbed the pocket of my brand new, hand-sewn, Hawaiian boy, palm-treed shirt and ripped it right off my chest. I had waited nearly a dad-blamed year for that shirt, and I am still trying to forgive him, today. To make matters worse, Lynda was not impressed.

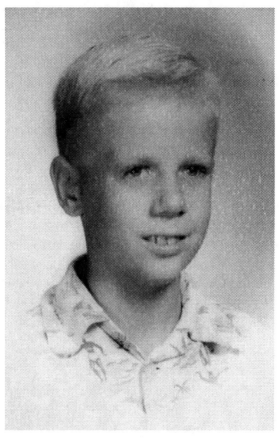

**My favorite shirt**

When I could find a dime, I'd head to Bill's store as quick as I could to check out all the different kinds of penny candy that filled the big, glass counter that was located at the very front of the store. I loved those Kitts, Mary Janes, BB Bats, and the long swirled pieces of licorice. You could get a dime's worth and be set for an hour or so. I really liked Fireballs, too. They were so hot; you had to keep taking them out of your mouth to give it a chance to cool off. We kids would dare each other to see who could keep their Fireballs in their mouths the longest. They were really popular and would last a long time. One of my all time favorite treats was a box of Cracker Jacks and it cost a whole nickel! There was a prize in every box and the prizes were a lot better then, than they are today. Those were really the "good ol' days."

Most candy bars were only a nickel then, but I remember when the new larger size, Baby Ruth candy bars became available. They weighed one fourth of a pound and cost an entire dime. Can you believe it? Today, the danged things are hardly more than a good-sized bite and cost nearly a dollar.

One memorable day, Roger bought one of those big Baby Ruths and opened it up to share it with me. He held that thing up in the air and broke it in half—right in front of me to prove his honesty. Well—wouldn't you know it—one half was bigger than the other? He said he couldn't help it, but he could fix it. He stuck the bigger piece of that peanut-laden, chocolate covered piece of heaven in his mouth and bit off a big chunk. He then held the two pieces up, side by side, so I could see that they were now even. Roger was always honest, but that solution still doesn't seem quite right to me!

Six Pepsi Colas or Cocoa-Colas came in reusable metal cartons and cost only twenty-five cents—plus the deposit, of course. I was tickled to death when Lotta Colas hit the market. Those suckers were a full sixteen ounces—Cokes were only six. Lotta Colas tasted like they were watered down a little bit, but there was a whole lot more to drink. I was out for quantity, not quality! When I was a kid, I was practically a bottomless pit. A Party-Pak was a popular drink for those who had money. Those things cost a quarter, but they had twenty-four ounces in them. I would have to save up to treat myself to a Party-Pak. Sometimes, Roger and I would go in together and split one. Heck, today, soft drinks are available in monstrous sizes for the big-bladdered people.

Daddy was still partial to the little six-ounce Cokes. When they raised the price of a Coke from a nickel to six cents each; Daddy declared, "That's the end of Cocoa-Cola". He still bought one once in a while though.

Sometimes, Laura would have one of her friends or our cousin, Geraldine Oliphant, to our house to spend the night with her. As I stated before, we never had a whole lot of money. When we got a twelve-ounce Pepsi, we had to share it. That was the law! There were three lines printed on the back of the Pepsi bottle. *Bottled under the Authority of* was printed on the first line, *The Pepsi Cola Bottling Company* on the second line, and *Winston Salem, North Carolina* on the third line. We Ketchie kids had already measured this thing several times and knew that the middle line was exactly half of that Pepsi-Cola. Well, Daddy popped some of our homegrown popcorn that evening and the Pepsis were passed around to us kids. We watched Geraldine intently as she drank swallow after swallow of that Pepsi. When she got down past that third line, I almost lost it! Roger and Laura were sharing a Pepsi between them and Geraldine was supposed to share hers with me! Nobody said anything, and she kept on drinking until she drank the entire Pepsi. She didn't know she had to pass it off to me. I never really got over it. I told her the whole story a few days ago, and she thought it was hilarious. She would—she got to drink the whole danged thing.

Bill Overcash's store was one of the few places that carried salt-fish. I remember that the fish came in a big wooden keg and Bill would always let Daddy know when he got some of it in stock. The fish were packed in salt to preserve them, so I guess that's why they called it salt-fish.

They were extremely salty, too. Daddy just loved them and what Daddy liked, is usually what we ate. It could have been worse—we could have had liver! I personally liked all kinds of fish but that stuff was a little too salty for my taste. I ate it anyway because when we had it for supper that was all we had.

Mama would often send me to Bill's store to get some DUZ detergent. She made sure that I got DUZ because they were sponsoring a big promotion that included a dish of some sort in each box of detergent. The dishes were really pretty and I think that we nearly completed an entire set. The dishes came in the Golden Wheat pattern with gold trim around the edges. It took a long time to get a set together because there might be a saucer in one box, a cup in another box, and a dinner plate in yet another. I know that this promotion induced Mama to buy a whole lot of DUZ because she would often send me to the store to see if any new shipments had arrived that would possibly have a dish in the box that she didn't have yet. It was fun and exciting to try to collect the entire set. Now the doggoned things are collector's items.

**Bill Overcash's store**

Bill Overcash's store changed ownership a couple of times but always provided a major presence in our community. I worked there years later when Mr. Ralph Thompson and his wife, Lois, ran it and sold Gulf gasoline. I learned a great deal from them and will always cherish the memories of my time spent working in their store. Before Mr. Thompson closed the store one Christmas Eve, he gathered a bunch of oranges, apples, nuts, and candy and put them in a big box. I had no idea why he was doing that because there were no customers in the store. He called me over to the side and handed me that big box of fruit and candy and said with a slight grin, "Merry Christmas". I was so excited I couldn't wait until I got home. That memory of his kindness will last a lifetime for this country boy. The store was torn down last year and now the Statesville Highway entrance to the Wynborne Housing Development passes right beside the store's original location.

Carl Harkey's store was like another home to me when I was growing up and I went there every chance I got. Carl's store is gone now, too. Just about all the old country stores that were around Mooresville have become victims of progress. You never hear of anyone hanging around one of those new convenience stores: pitching horseshoes, playing cards, checkers, or mumble-peg.

Many friends were made at those humble, country stores and they were always there when we needed them. I really miss them all.

# Dining with the Ketchies

Dining with the Ketchies was sometimes considered a unique experience. There was never a dull moment at our table or at Grandma's table either. Daddy cooked most of our meals after Mama started working in the cotton mill and would only call us <u>one</u> time for supper. He would yell, "Let's eat. Let's eat, 'fore I throw it in the creek." We kids would come running when we heard that supper call.

There were not many kinds of food that I didn't like to eat. I was raised "Country", but still, I had my limits. I never liked beef liver. I never liked it then, and I don't like it now. I remember one particular evening when we were having liver and onions and homemade biscuits. Picking the entrée for our evening meal was not up to me or I would definitely not have chosen liver. I was prepared to just eat a biscuit.

I remember this incident like it happened just yesterday. Mama and Daddy strongly encouraged me try some of the liver. They insisted that it was good for me since it had a whole lot of iron in it. Who likes to eat iron—for God's sake? Not me! Their encouraging didn't work too well; so they got down to demanding that I try the nasty stuff. I kept telling them that I didn't like the way it smelled, the way it looked, or the texture of it. I tried my best to convince them that, if I even tasted it, I would throw up. They wouldn't listen to the words of a wise youth, and they paid the consequences. Daddy made me load up a big forkful and try it anyway. As soon as that liver hit my tongue, I started throwing up all over the table and what seemed like, half the kitchen. The table was declared a disaster area, the meal declared officially over, and I declared that I would never eat liver again. I don't think that Daddy declared anything at all—but, I think he might have cussed a little bit.

If anyone reading these memoirs wishes to invite me to share a meal with them, please note, "I will not eat liver!"

As a rule, we ate pretty well. Sometimes, however, we would just have cornbread and buttermilk or just cold biscuits and regular milk. We got our milk from Grandma's cows and it was the real thing—not the watered down, homogenized stuff that came from the grocery store. That whole milk didn't make me like those meals any better. Mama never fixed anything special for any of us kids. You ate what was set before you or you didn't eat. It was that simple. Sometimes I just wouldn't eat.

Daddy tried to get us to believe that crumbled up biscuits in milk was a real treat. I was already questioning the wisdom in some of Daddy's opinions and this was one of those times. We fed our old dog, Snooks, biscuits that were crumbled-up in milk for her supper just about everyday. I thought I was a little more important than our dog. I guess I was more important, but that didn't change what we had for supper. I realize now that we couldn't afford fancy meals and sometimes that was all we had.

**Snooks, the biscuit eater, and me**

I always wondered why Snooks looked so sad. I guess it was because all she had to eat was just crumbled-up, old biscuits and milk.

Daddy had taught Laura how to make biscuits, and that was one way she could help out at suppertime. She became very adept at this biscuit-making job and always made about fifty-five or sixty biscuits for every meal. You have to remember there were five of us that would be eating them. Heck, Laura used to eat twelve of the things herself. The biscuits were not very large—we used a small, Pet Evaporated Milk can as a biscuit cutter.

Well, one slow, uneventful day was dragging on when Laura came up with a brilliant idea. She said, "Why don't we make some coffeecakes?" Well, anything with the "cake" word in it got my attention. Laura only knew how to make about sixty biscuits at a time. I guess she could have cut the recipe in half, but it just didn't occur to her. She mixed up all that dough, I cut the biscuits out, and rolled them in melted butter and brown sugar. I finally got them all rolled and coated and Laura put them in the oven—one pan at a time. It took a lot of pans!

The two of us made a sizable dent in the coffeecake inventory. Laura and I ate about twenty-five or thirty of them while they were still hot. (We didn't want to spoil our supper.) Roger wasn't home to help us eat up the last thirty of the coffeecakes, and we didn't want to get caught wasting bread dough; so we hit the road, trying to give them to the neighbors. We ended the whole affair by eating another fifteen or twenty by ourselves and giving the rest of them to our dog, Snooks. Those coffeecakes were really good, but I don't think I've had one since.

If it were not for pinto beans and good old, Irish potatoes, I don't think I would have made it to adolescence. I would dive into a plate of pinto beans and onions with the gusto of a hound dog. Sopping up the bean juice with cornbread that Mama made in the iron skillet was a real treat.

I didn't mind getting my iron from a skillet, but I'll be danged if I was going to get it from eating liver. We always had cornbread when we had pinto beans—it might have been a written doctrine that was part of our Southern heritage, I don't know. They just belonged together.

We ate lots and lots of potatoes. We ate them boiled, stewed, mashed, fried, and made into soup. I even ate potatoes raw when I was peeling them because, half the time, I couldn't wait for supper. Sometimes, Mama even mixed them with onions and made fried potato patties. I never did care for onions mixed in with my "taters". Daddy used a lot of potatoes in his homemade vegetable soup. He would make soup by the gallons. The more vegetables he added into it, the better I liked it. We called the vegetables "guts".

When Grandma dipped soup out of the pot and into our bowls, she would always ask, "Do you want soup or guts?" It made sense to me!

Well, I remember having a friend come home from school with me one day to play in Grandma's pasture. Grandma always said that we had to get our name in the "pot" if we were going to eat with them; so I told her that my guest and I would have supper with them. That evening, Grandma was having homemade vegetable soup. Hers was always a little thinner than Daddy's and sometimes she would have to go fishing just to find the vegetables. Well, we were all sitting around the table that night for supper; and Grandma was into her soup-dipping mode when she came to my friend and asked, "Soup or guts?" I thought the poor boy was going to break and run.

You never knew what you were going to find on Grandma's supper table. One time we caught a big turtle, and Uncle Gordon fixed it for supper. We thought we were dining in high style. It really tasted good and was different from anything that we had ever had before. But, the thing that really got my attention was when they had big, yellow, chicken feet (toenails and all) sitting in a large bowl on the dining room table—just like it was normal. It was definitely not normal for me. I couldn't make myself eat one of those nasty looking things if my life depended on it.

Fried chicken legs, (not feet), were always one of my favorite dishes. We raised our own chickens but still didn't have meat on the table very often. I often say in jest, "We were going to have chicken for dinner one Sunday, but it got well." We really didn't have it that bad, but I was always hungry.

Before we could eat the chicken we had to catch the thing and wring its neck. I despised killing chickens and there's one incident that stands out in the "chicken-killing" chapter of my life.

I was afraid of them to begin with because they always pecked me and it hurt like the dickens. I also didn't like them flapping their wings when I was trying to catch one of the fast-running, two-legged, feathered fowls. I liked it even less when I finally caught one. I watched Roger as he deftly grabbed a chicken by the neck and wrung it round and round until he was sure it was dead. He then laid it on the ground and the poor thing flopped around in the yard a little bit and finally quit moving. Well, I tried to do the same thing to my chicken, but my hand was too small and I evidently never got a good grip. I wrung that blasted thing round and round just like Roger did, but when mine hit the ground, he ran around like he was drunk for a while and then just took off for parts unknown. I don't know why in the world we couldn't have just shot'em and been done with the whole ordeal.

I think I hated plucking the feathers about as much as I hated killing them. Mama would dip those dead chickens down into some scalding water to make the feathers turn loose and then we would pick the feathers out one-by-one until the chicken was completely naked. Next, we took a brown paper bag, set it afire, and held it under the chicken to singe any remaining feathers off the poor thing. In spite of doing all this distasteful stuff to the chicken, I still couldn't wait to eat the poor sucker.

Daddy would often make squirrel dumplings for us in the wintertime. Roger and I brought home a lot of squirrels during hunting season, and Daddy would cook them and serve them with homemade dumplings. It made a great diversion from our normal meals. We ate lots of rabbits, too. We ate rabbits fried, stewed, and barbecued.

I was recently talking about eating rabbits at church one night and it became evident that my friend Kandi Hauser had never eaten one. She asked, "What does rabbit taste like?" Without thinking, I replied, "It tastes a lot like squirrel." Heck, I thought that everybody had at least eaten a squirrel—evidently everybody hasn't! Well, I thought Kandi, her husband Steve and their children would never stop laughing. I realized then, there's a possibility that I am a little more country than I thought.

One of Daddy's specialties was catfish stew and he would make gallons of it at a time. He had to; we ate gallons of it at a time. We would invite David Wilson over when we had catfish stew or frog legs. David was always with us when we caught the fish or the frogs and it was only fitting that he share in the feast. He was like another member of our family. In fact, when Daddy passed away, David rode in the family car with us.

Most of the time, we had cornmeal mush and sausage for breakfast. If we were lucky, we would have country ham and red-eye gravy with our mush. I thought rich people ate grits and we poor folks had to eat mush. Uncle Gordon would often pour some of his mush into a glass of milk and eat it. Like I said before, I had my limits—pouring mush into my milk and eating it with a spoon was beyond any of those limits.

One time, when Laura had a friend spending the night with her, Mama felt obligated to be a little fancy. The next morning, we gathered around the table for breakfast, and right smack-dab in the middle of our kitchen table sat a big bowl of mush. I had lived in our house a good number of years by then and had never seen anything like that before. The mush had always been poured right out of the pot straight onto our plates. Now I had a dad-blamed extra bowl to wash. Mush was still mush to me, regardless of what it was in, or how we got it to our plates. I really didn't think the bowl hid the fact that it was still just plain old mush.

Daddy often had to go to Charlotte for skin cancer treatments. When he did, we would stop at the Tip Top Bakery Outlet on the way home and buy eight or ten loaves of day-old bread for ten cents a loaf. We usually put some of the loaves in the freezer. We didn't have an electric toaster back then, so we just put ten or twelve slices of bread at a time on a baking sheet and slid it the under the broiler in the oven.

We liked having toast for breakfast and would eat an entire loaf of bread at one meal. We always had homemade grape and blackberry jellies or strawberry preserves to spread on our toast. It was really a nice change from having mush everyday.

Daddy was in the Army during World War II, and I think some of his training stuck with him. He liked order at the table when we were eating. There were also certain duties required of us kids, but Daddy's clues were sometimes fraught with ambiguity. (His clues weren't very clear.) I eventually learned that when he rattled ice around in his glass, he wanted one of us to get up and refill it with water. The sink was directly behind my chair, and this duty usually fell to me.

He liked for us to behave at the table, too. I tried hard; I really did! One night, I was told, in no uncertain terms, to be quiet. Sometimes I had trouble grasping the meaning of definitive suggestions. I guess you could say I didn't listen well. It was not that I didn't care; I just couldn't help myself.

Daddy sat directly across the table from me and would thump me on the top of my head like he was thumping a watermelon to see if it was ripe. Daddy had to do this quite often to further my education in table manners.

That night when he tried to give me a thump, I leaned back out of the way just enough to make him miss. He didn't appreciate my agility very much and picked up his table knife by the blade and was going to give me a real good thump with the handle. Daddy had done that before, and that usually got my attention. Well, when he thumped me with it this time, he connected solidly with my hard head causing the handle to fly off the knife and land in the sink. Well, the knife handle was pretty heavy, and it chipped the enamel on the sink. Then, Mama got mad at me, but Daddy was the one who was doing the thumping. It was really amazing, when I was young, how some simple things just got out of hand.

Mama went to work in the mill and Daddy stayed home with us kids and assumed the cooking duties and ran the household. One day, we talked him into making a chocolate cake for us. The layers came out perfectly and smelled terrific. I didn't even want to wait for the cake to be iced. I was ready to eat it like it was, while it was still warm. Daddy wasn't confident he could make the icing, but he whipped up a batch and started spreading it on the cake. Everything was looking pretty good until the layers began slipping and sliding. I think the icing was a little too thin and it was not holding the layers in place like, thick, creamy icing did. Daddy finally finished icing the cake but the top layer started sliding off to one side again, so he finally put the whole dad-gummed thing in the refrigerator to see if that would help. I think the cold air was just what it needed.

We waited for Mama to get home from the mill before we brought that sucker out of the refrigerator. The cake looked mighty impressive to me. We were all excited and proud of Daddy for making this beautiful chocolate cake. I thumped the top of the cake with my finger, and it sounded like an over-ripe watermelon, but I didn't say anything.

Daddy got a knife from the drawer and commenced cutting the first slice for Mama, but the doggoned knife-blade wouldn't penetrate the icing. I guess it set up too much while in the refrigerator. Daddy was determined to cut the cake, so he tried using a bigger, sharper knife to try and make some headway through the icing. He finally jabbed the sharp point of the knife straight down into the top of the cake with both hands, and that did the trick. The cake really tasted good and was a great success. We all got a good laugh out of the whole situation. It's really hard to mess up a chocolate cake and we kids would have eaten it regardless what it looked like.

Daddy made the best carrot cake that I have ever eaten. He would gather hickory nuts from our tree and take them to the woodworking shop and crack them with a hammer and dig the goodies out of their stubborn shells. He always used hickory nuts in his carrot cake. I don't know if that was what made them so wonderful or not, but they were really special. Squirrels would come up to him when he was cracking the hickory nuts and eat right out of his hand. Daddy always had a way with animals—it was his two-legged offspring that gave him the most trouble.

Mama could cook, too and her specialty was making "stickies". They were nothing but bread dough that had been rolled out really thin, and then covered with hunks of butter and loads of white sugar. The whole thing would then be rolled up to resemble a white log. Then Mama would slice that log and fit the swirls of dough into baking pans and pop them in the oven. Invariably, there would be a fight amongst us Ketchie kids to see who would get the first pan. It was all I could do to eat two or three pans full by myself. I would give ten dollars; no make that twenty, to have a pan or two of Mama's "stickies" right now.

We didn't have much money; but by golly, we ate pretty doggoned well, considering. I would give just about anything to sit around the table and share a meal with all my folks again. For that great opportunity, I might even try some liver and let Daddy have a free "thump".

# Brown's Skating Rink and Swimming Pool

Each summer would seem hotter than the last one, and if we didn't have our own little stream dammed up for a pond, we would head for Brown's Pool.

Mr. Brown had placed a sign on the Mt. Ulla Highway that pointed the way down a beautiful, winding lane that disappeared around a curve through some woods. The road wound steeply the last few yards down a big hill to the parking area. It was really a romantic setting when you saw it all unfold before your eyes. There was a rippling stream, spanned by a quaint wooden footbridge that led to the pool and the skating rink. The entire complex was surrounded by beautiful woods. A large gazebo was situated beside the rink and was available for picnics. Every structure was painted a light shade of royal blue. Four or five swings were situated near the steps that led inside the rink where most of the action took place.

**The pool, rink and pond**

The entire setting was really beautiful, and I thought I was in a different world when I was there. It's hard to believe that it was only about a mile-and-a-half or two miles from my home. Mr. Frank Brown, along with his wife, Nell, and their children, Buddy and Martha, ran the entire enterprise.

The pool was fed by an extremely cold spring, located in the woods behind their skating rink. That crystal clear water was pure—no chlorine was ever added to it. I don't care how hot the weather was, the water always felt as if someone filled the pool with a ton of ice. The pool was made out of concrete and had some rough places that would hurt tender feet. We went barefoot at the first signs of spring and by the time summer came around our feet were tough enough for us to walk on just about anything. The pool was a terrific place to cool off after a hard day of loading sacks of wheat on the wagon or hauling hay.

**Cooling off in Brown's Pool**

Sometimes, Roger and I were fortunate enough to be asked to drain Brown's Pool, sweep it as clean as possible, and fill it again. Roger, being the oldest, elected himself to be the one who dived from the board, swam down to the bottom, and opened the drain. I could have dived off the board myself but I wasn't strong enough to turn the valve; so I just let him do it. Anyway, it made him happy to know he was in charge. It would take him a few times, while holding his breath as long as he could, to accomplish the job.

Once the water had been drained, the entire pool had to be swept by hand and all the trash that had accumulated on the bottom of the pool had to be picked up and carried away. Then, Roger would close the drain so the water could start filling it again. It took several hours to complete the job and we received no monetary compensation—but we got to swim all summer for free. You talk about a good deal! It really was for us.

All of us country kids could swim pretty well and were accomplished at "ducking" one another and swimming off as fast as we could before the other one had a chance to do the same thing to us. The Brown's didn't allow much horsing around at their pool, but my favorite thing was to run off the diving board with great speed and performing my fantastic "cannonball". (They kind of frowned on the cannonball thing.) I would mainly do it to splash the older, teenage girls that were sunning themselves around the edge of the pool. I was a regular nuisance, but I had a lot of fun. I don't think my "cannonball" impressed the girls too much—I didn't see any of them waiting in line for my autograph.

The skating rink was situated just to the left of the pool. Laura and I would save our money and hope we would have enough to go skating on Thursday nights. Mama and Daddy would usually let us go if we were able catch a ride. Sometimes, Phyllis, Carolyn, and J.C. Curtis would take us and bring us back home. I think Laura was kind of sweet on J. C. and the feeling might have been mutual. He never did cut any back-flips when he found out I was tagging along. I don't remember Daddy or Mama ever taking us. When they were in for the night—they were in!

The wintertime was something else. The pool was closed and drained, of course; but the rink was a beehive of activity. Martha was always patient with me even though she had to take my skates off and put them back on each time I had to go outside to the toilet. The skates were the old adjustable ones that had to be fitted right on our shoes. I finally saved enough money to buy a used pair of shoe skates. They were a little too big, but I was proud to have them just the same. Having someone else put my skates on for me always made me feel a little self-conscious. I was twelve or thirteen years old by then, maybe even a little older.

There was a huge pot-bellied stove in the left corner of the rink that was surrounded by a wooden rail. Sometimes that old stove would be red hot! It was supposed to heat the entire rink, but it never did. I would bravely make a couple of rounds before racing back to the rail and leaning over as far as I could to warm myself. You could only warm one side of yourself at a time when you were standing right beside the blasted thing. I could have climbed around the railing and sat on the bench that was next to the stove, but I seldom took the time.

I was always scared of girls and was really bashful when I was around them. Occasionally, I would get up enough nerve to skate with one of them, but when I'd start thinking about how cute she was—I usually fell on my rear end, taking her down with me. It was really embarrassing. After all, I was a great skater in my own eyes. Causing them to fall usually postponed any of my romantic attempts for a while.

However, sometimes I would sit in one of the swings, that was outside the rink, with a girl my age or a little younger. I only sat with ones that I knew or wanted to know better. Pat Cowan and Vickey Edmiston were two of my favorite friends of the female persuasion, and I felt fairly comfortable around them. We would often skate together and listen to the same old organ music, lap after lap. I was pretty proud of my skating ability and sometimes skated backwards while holding hands with one of the young ladies. It wasn't until I was in high school that I felt a little more comfortable around the opposite sex. I didn't know what I had missed—but I was pretty sure I had missed a lot.

**Brown's Skating Rink and Swimming Pool**

The entire Brown family was extremely patient with all of us young people but did not tolerate any misbehavior. I was called down for "skating too fast" a few times. That was one way I tried to impress the girls. I heard they liked fast cars; and since I didn't drive, "fast skates" was the best I could do. We weren't allowed to "pop the whip", either. It usually ended up being a huge calamity, anyway.

Some of the fondest memories of my childhood are of the days and nights spent at Brown's Rink and Pool. I sure wish they were still there. I would really like to go down that little lane that wound through the woods just one more time and hold hands with a pretty girl while sitting in one of the swings. Maybe I would even have nerve enough to kiss her now.

# Going to Town

Downtown Mooresville was a bustling place in the early 1950's, and finding a place to park was a real problem. Mother would often have to park on Broad Street, in front of Hobb's Cleaners, cross the railroad track at Moore Avenue, and then walk to Main Street. Mama was a beautiful woman, and I can still picture her in my mind, walking south on Broad Street while wearing her white dress that had small red flowers printed on it. The dress had a full skirt that flowed in the breeze as she walked.

We didn't get to go to town very often, but when we did, we tried to make the most of it. However, the offspring of Helen and Bob Ketchie were a pretty rowdy bunch and had to stay in the car the majority of the time. Sometimes we argued or fought just like brothers and sisters. I think it was good for Mama to have a little time of her own and get away from us kids for a while. Sometimes when she returned, she would have a candy bar for us to share. If we had been good and had not beaten up on each other while she was gone, she would let us eat it.

There were two department stores on Main Street: Belk's and Raylass. Mama usually shopped at Raylass because their merchandise was less expensive than Belk's. I remember Raylass having a big, wide staircase going up the right side of the building, just as you entered the front door. I was always impressed with stairs and couldn't wait to climb them.

However, I remember Belk's Department Store pretty well, too. It had black, marble-looking stuff on the front of it and there were two or three entrances. Belk's had an elevator that was operated by a black lady, Marie Bailey. She would close the metal-accordion door and ask what floor you needed; then she would push the button for you. I thought that was the neatest thing. There were only three levels in the entire store, but I guess they didn't want anybody to get lost.

**Belk's Department Store 1950's**

Belk's Department Store had a big toy department on the third floor. I would wander among the toy displays and wish for things that I would probably never get. I remember a badminton set displayed on a high shelf, out of reach of kids like me. I would just stare and stare at that box until I had everything about it memorized. The blue-green box had a picture across the front of people playing badminton. The box was about three feet long and over a foot wide. I really coveted that badminton set with all of my little, ten-year-old heart. I knew I would probably never get to play tennis, but if I could just get one of those badminton sets, that would be close enough.

You know what? Santa Claus brought a badminton set to me for Christmas that year and it was just like the one I saw in Belk's. Everything was exactly as I remembered. It even had the Belk's price sticker on the side of the box. I was surprised that Santa Claus shopped at Belk's too.

Belk's also sold boy's shoes that had spring-loaded tongues that folded down over your feet. The shoes came fully equipped with tractor-cleats on the bottom. I think every boy in Shepherd School had a pair of those shoes with the tractor-cleat soles, so naturally I wanted a pair, too. I also wanted those new shoes because you didn't have to tie them—I always seemed to have a problem keeping my shoes tied. Raylass didn't have anything even close to the latest in high-fashioned footwear for boys! Raylass had Oxfords, and Mama always wanted me to get those—whatever Oxfords were.

I finally talked Mama into getting the super-cool shoes with the tractor cleats for me. I think she just got tired of hearing me whine. The honeymoon was soon over between those shoes and me. The red mud would get stuck between the cleats something terrible; and I would, of course, track the mud all over the house. Mama didn't care for that at all! I would have to sit on the back steps, take a Popsicle stick, and scrape the mud out from in between the cleats. I hated having to do this manual labor stuff, and Mama absolutely refused to do it. Asking Daddy to do it for me was out of the question, and I couldn't talk Roger or Laura into helping me, either; so I ended up having to do it myself. I learned a valuable lesson from those things. I only got that one pair of tractor-cleat shoes in my whole life, and I was never able to talk Mama into much again after that. I let her pick my shoes from then on, too.

Downtown Mooresville was a busy place in the 1950's. There were three movie theaters, several restaurants, two or three barbershops, a bowling alley, and two major taxi stands. Belk's Department Store was the main attraction, but there were at least three furniture stores, Delk's 5&10, plus a Roses' and Raylass. City Grocery and Market and Mayhew-McNeely Grocery were on Main Street, too, and they delivered groceries to their customers all over town. Two or three jewelry stores and several second floor doctors' offices filled the shopping area to overflowing. The Harris-Teeter Supermarket chain had its humble beginnings on Main Street in Mooresville. It was called only Teeters then—it became Harris-Teeters many years later. Of course, there were banks, too; and they all stayed open on Saturday.

One of my favorite places to visit was D. E. Turner Hardware. Mr. Elmer Turner always lifted me up to the gumball machine and put a penny in for me. I still remember the thrill I got every time I watched the gumball roll out of the glass dome, down a little track, and right into my waiting hand. The hardware store has been in Mooresville since 1895.

**Looking north on Main Street, 1957**

Mooresville was mainly a textile town and the majority of its inhabitants worked in one of the cotton mills. Mooresville Mills was located on the south end of town and naturally became known as the Lower Mill. It was the largest of them all and ended its first shift every afternoon at 3:00. Town would fill up in a hurry with mill-workers, scurrying around, shopping for groceries, and whatever else they needed.

Saturdays brought almost a festive air to town. The smell of popcorn from the theaters and the hotdogs from the restaurants permeated the air. I could hardly stand it! (A robust appetite seems to be about the only thing that I never outgrew.) I remember when you could buy twelve hot dogs for a dollar when they were on special. Sometimes, Daddy would buy a dozen, but that was never enough for all of us. I recall later, as prices rose, Minute Grill sold them at eight for a dollar. I was working then and I would buy eight hot dogs, sit right there, and eat every one of them. They fixed them the right way, too: mustard next to the dog, then slaw, and then chili on the top. It never got any better than that. Eight hot dogs were about my limit because I had to have two Pepsis to wash them down, and I didn't want to spoil my supper.

I had heard about "loafers" before but thought they had something to do with shoes. I found out later that the men I saw leaning against the side of the corner bank, soaking up the sun, were also called loafers. There was also a bunch of them that hung around the taxi stands. My mama would always grab my hand as we approached these places where the men hung out. I guess she thought if she hurried me by them that I wouldn't learn any bad habits. I didn't see anything wrong with just hanging around, doing nothing; I would have liked to have done that myself.

There were two or three taxi stands in Mooresville and I thought that they were pretty special. I hitched a ride in a taxi one time out in front of our house. The taxi driver took me all the way to town and didn't even charge me a dime. I thought he was really a nice man. He drove for Flip's Taxi and might have been Mr. Flip himself.

Flip's Taxi was on the north end of the business section in front of an old garage. It had a big covered porch that jutted out to the street. Smith's Taxi was down a few blocks south, beside Blackwelder's Furniture Company. George Malcolm later opened George's Taxi beside the State Theater. All of them were on Main Street and seemed to do a good business.

**George's Taxi**

Roger and I would often hitch a ride to town on Saturday night to see a movie, and then walk the railroad track back home. One night, a train came while we were in an area where the bushes, briars, and weeds grew tall on both sides of the track. Finding an escape route was not easy and I just froze and couldn't move. Roger grabbed my hand and dragged me down the embankment, through the bushes and briars to safety. It was a good thing he was with me, or I might not be here today. As one old fellow used to say, "That really scared my mule!"

Directly in front of Cook's Grocery at the intersection of Patterson Avenue, Statesville Avenue, and Broad Street is where Southern Railway split the railroad tracks. We called this place "The Junction". The eastern track went to Winston-Salem, and the northern fork ran parallel along Statesville Highway and went right by our house. Sometimes Daddy would pull the car over on to the shoulder of the road in front of Cook's Grocery so we could watch the men fill the train with coal and water. Then, we would race home so I could get out in the front yard and wave at the train as it passed.

**My painting of Cook's Grocery**

You could hear that old steam engine coming from a long ways off. The smoke would be pouring from its stack and the drive wheels would be churning and vibrating the ground in our whole neighborhood. I would wave and give the engineer the "sign" to blow the horn. I always thought that he blew the horn just for me because I was so cute and he couldn't resist my winning smile. I found out later there was a whistle post in front of Mr. Blackwelder's house, and the engineer didn't have a choice—he had to blow the horn. (It was a "railroad law".) Nonetheless, he always waved back at me and that made me feel really special.

The movie theaters were real special places. The smell of popcorn hit you as soon as you went through the door, and there were all kinds of photographs and movie posters that lined the walls on both sides of the entrance. It was always fun to look at them and try to figure out what the movie was going to be about.

However, we didn't go to the inside movie theaters very often. You had to wear shoes in most of them. If you didn't, you would get chewing gum stuck all over the bottoms of your feet. I hated that! The candy was always overpriced, too; and I didn't like that either.

We went to the drive-in theaters instead. Sometimes Daddy took us to the Carolina Drive-In on Wednesday nights. It was located at the intersection of Highway 150 and Highway 152. You could take a whole carload to see a double feature and two cartoons for a dollar. Now that was a deal! We would pop a huge, paper grocery bag plumb full of popcorn, fill a gallon jar with water, and we were set. Often, we would invite one of our cousins or a friend to come along. As soon as we got there, we kids would pile out of the car and sit on a blanket on the ground or on one of the car's fenders.

The Mooresville-Davidson Drive-In Theater was located south of Mount Mourne on Highway 115. We didn't go there very often because it was much farther away. We usually just went to the Carolina—it was closer and had "Dollar Night".

Daddy always enjoyed any Abbott and Costello movie. We were watching *African Screams* one night, and I crawled down behind Daddy's seat when a lion got after Lou Costello. I thought that all the stuff I saw in the movies was real and Lou was going to be eaten by the lion. The night scenes always scared me, too and I was always glad when daylight returned and the danger had passed.

All of us really liked Westerns the best, and Mama liked anything that was in Technicolor. It didn't make much difference to me what kind of movie was playing as long as I got to go. May the truth be told, I really didn't like scary movies—I mainly just wanted to see some cartoons more than anything else.

Being without much financial clout made dating at the drive-in theater a really good bargain. Hot dogs were fifteen cents, popcorn was a dime, and it only cost a dollar to get in. Besides; it was also a convenient place for some stolen kisses. I didn't actually steal any kisses but I borrowed quite a few. The kind young ladies in my company always seemed to want me to pay them back—I happily obliged.

I remember one summer evening in particular when the Carolina Drive-In had a Road Runner cartoon night. (That was all that was on.) I laughed so hard that I started coughing and was overcome with an acute attack of asthma right there. All the mouth-to-mouth resuscitation that my date provided was still not sufficient to make my breathing easier. I had to take my date home before we had any hot dogs. Talk about a bummer.

Those were still the good old days. I think that the drive-in theater is the place where I officially got over my bashfulness.

# Shepherd School Days

1950 was a memorable year for this little, white-headed boy. I was sent off to school for the first time. There was no free kindergarten available for us country kids. We did not pass GO; we did not collect $200; we went directly to big-time school.

**Dear old Shepherd School**

I think Shepherd School was built sometime in the late 1920's. It was a fairly modern, brick schoolhouse—as far as schoolhouses go. I didn't give a rat's hat what kind of school I was going to be housed in; I didn't want to go! I would rather have stayed home and played with my little cars and trucks. Roger and Laura assured me that everything would be all right if I just stayed with them.

I remember that September morning when the old number "14" bus stopped right in front of our house. I was herded along with Pat and Donnie Lambert, Hal Blackwelder, Joe Ketchie, Roger, and Laura as we boarded that intimidating vehicle for my first day of school. Well, that alone was enough to scare a six-year old country kid half to death. Everyone on that bus, but us, was disguised as strangers. I was out of my element here, folks! They all looked at this puny, little, white-headed kid and wondered if I was even old enough to be going to school in the first place.

There were benches fitted along each side of the bus and one big, long bench going right down the middle. When our bus driver, Geraldine Craven, stopped a little too abruptly, everybody slid on his or her rear end, all the way to the front of the bus. That helped me get to know some of the other kids almost immediately because the sudden stop jammed us all together at the ends of the benches.

We stopped at Carl Harkey's store and in front of Kilroy's Service Station to pick up the majority of the rest of our load. I think there were about nineteen Overcash kids that boarded the bus at that one stop in front of Kilroy's store.

The schoolhouse was only about another mile up the road from there, so the remainder of the trip was pretty much uneventful. Geraldine pulled into the circular driveway of Shepherd School and opened the door for us to disembark and I began a new chapter in my life.

We all piled out of the bus for our first day of the 1950-1951 school year and were greeted by none other than our illustrious principal, Mr. Charlie Clark.

Mr. Clark was a nice looking man, dressed in a suit, hat, and necktie. I found out pretty soon that he was "The Man" and he was in charge. He was pointing here and there, telling us kids where to go. You know, people sometimes still tell me where to go.

Anyway, Mr. Clark directed us little first graders to our class. As we went by his office, I remembered hearing about his paddle, with holes drilled in it so he could gain more momentum when giving you a whipping. I decided then, not to mess with "The Man".

**My first principal, Mr. Charlie Clark**

Roger and Laura <u>did</u> leave me, even after they told me they wouldn't. They lied! I didn't know bean dip about school, and I thought that I might get to stay with them and follow them around all day. Well, folks, that never happened!

I was soon ushered into a classroom filled with long, wood tables that had six chairs set around each one. There were holes cut in the sides of the table, right in front of each of the chairs. This nice, little, gray-haired lady pointed me to a particular seat, and I took it—not wanting to be a troublemaker or anything. I had no idea what those holes were used for but was soon to learn. Later, I was given a tablet with big lines drawn on each page. I was supposed to keep my tablet in the hole in the table where I was sitting. I had no idea what I had gotten myself into, and I wanted to go home something terrible. Daddy had already instructed me that I would get another whipping at home if I was to get one at school and I was determined to behave.

I sat down between two boys that I had never seen in my whole life. The little fellow on one side of me said, "Hey, my name is George Bailey. What's yours?" Since he was so nice to me, I felt obligated to tell him. I timidly said, "Millard."

Well, George didn't say a doggoned thing about my name being funny or anything. I had already dodged one bullet and hadn't even been at school fifteen minutes. The boy on the other side of the table seemed nice, too. He said, "Hey, my name is Jerry Waugh."

I liked these two boys right off, and telling them my name didn't embarrass me nearly as much as I thought it would. Maybe this school stuff wasn't going to be so bad after all. I had never seen so many new faces in one place in all my life. I figured that I would now have lots of kids to play with that were my own age. Before going to school, I only knew one person my age, and that was my first cousin, Danny Wilhelm, and he would sometimes beat up on me.

I found out later that the little, gray-haired lady was Mrs. Essie Smith. She told us we could call her Mrs. Smith, and I thought that was pretty reasonable since I didn't know her personally.

George; Jerry; and my cousin, Danny Wilhelm, were all at my table. I think David Smith and Gary Ervin were also seated with us. We all got along really well and became good friends. There were a lot of pretty girls in my class too, but I was really shy and didn't talk to very many of them. I remember a dark-haired boy in our class who ate those big, lead pencils that first graders always used. I tried one but didn't like it worth a hoot. He constantly had black smudges all around his mouth from the lead, and it really wasn't a pretty sight.

I soon found out that I liked to talk a lot. In fact, I talked too much! I remember Mrs. Smith telling all of us to be quiet. Lord; that was hard for me to do. I didn't take her suggestion very seriously and just kept talking to George Bailey as if she had never said a word. The next thing I knew, that woman popped me upside my head so fast I didn't know what hit me. I remember that I cried and cried and laid my head down on my arms. I guess I went to sleep because the next thing I remember was good ole George rubbing my head and assuring me that everything was going to be OK.

I dodged another bullet when I got home that night. Daddy and Mama had been sent a note from Mrs. Smith about "the incident". Well, Daddy, being the reasonable man that he was, thought that the punishment I had received at school was sufficient and decided to let it go since this was my first day at school. I heartily agreed with him and didn't question his wisdom pertaining to corporal punishment. You know, I never got a single whipping at school that year. Mrs. Smith taught me well about the finer points of school discipline. When it came to being quiet; or getting a pop upside the head—the choice was not that difficult. Once was enough for this little boy.

There was a kind lady named Mrs. Rietzel who came from the Iredell County Health Department each year to check on all of us kids. I guess she wanted to know if we were healthy or if there was anything bothering us. To tell you the truth, I don't know what she did for sure, but she did give us a tiny cup of orange juice and a Lemon Thin cookie. I thought I had died and gone to Heaven when I tasted that cookie. As I remember, I had never had orange juice before, and that cookie was to die for. The main problem that I had with the whole setup was that I only got one of those wonderful little cookies. It wasn't very big, either; and I could have eaten at least fifty of those little suckers. Boy, they were good!

Recess and lunch were the best part of each day. They let us go outside for a few minutes in the morning and again in the afternoon. We even got to take a nap after lunch. I didn't mind that at all.

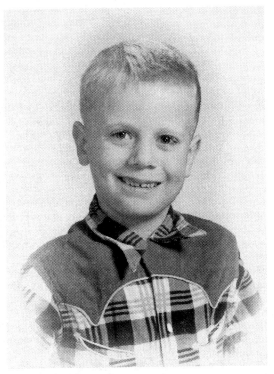

**My first grade picture**

The school had our pictures taken by a professional photographer. I remember wearing my cowboy shirt with little pockets that looked like "smiles". I still had all my baby teeth, and was grinning like a possum. The picture of me looked pretty doggoned good, if I do have to be the one to say so.

I learned my ABC's and began to read and print words. I learned a whole bunch of useful stuff that very first year. We read about some kids named Dick, Sally, and Jane, and their dog Spot. I don't remember anything about their parents or even if they had any. There were a bunch of books written about them, though; and it was evident that somebody thought a lot of them. I also learned to count to twenty or higher before I got too confused. I liked the first grade much better than I thought I would and made all A's on my report card.

I fell in love about every six months while in elementary school. However, it didn't do a whole lot of good. I always thought that Lynda Wilhelm was an especially attractive young member of the opposite sex. I probably would have died in the fourth grade if she were ever to have kissed me. I was pretty sure that her amorous attentions were aimed toward Jerry Waugh or David Smith. Seeing that I didn't have much of a chance, I just let it go. I was too bashful anyway, and I always thought I was so ugly, that Mama had to tie a pork chop around my neck, just so our dog would play with me.

By the fourth grade I was getting used to the school grind. At recess, we could buy a snack or ice cream if we had any money. I never did! I don't know where in the world Danny Wilhelm got his money: but I will never forget the day he bought me a Drumstick. A Drumstick was not your ordinary ice cream treat. It had a scoop of vanilla ice cream that was placed on a waffle cone, then dipped in chocolate, and finally covered with roasted peanuts. It was about the best thing I had ever tasted. The Drumstick cost Danny a whole dime, too. Maybe he still felt guilty about ripping my favorite Hawaiian shirt off my back and costing me the love of my life.

During the winter months, I would visit the cozy boiler room in the basement where our janitor, Lewis Caldwell, kept the fire going so that we could stay nice and warm. Lewis was a real congenial black man that all of us students loved and respected. It was somewhat comforting, sitting and talking to him; while listening to the steam rise to the radiator pipes. I remember the smell of coal and steam even today. Lewis always had a sympathetic ear for all of us younger kids and would listen to our problems. He was kind of a surrogate guidance counselor. We didn't have one at school in those days; but our teachers, Mr. Clark and Lewis Caldwell helped all of us adjust to the life of academia.

Fourth-Grade Class At Shepherd School, 1953-54

**My fourth grade class**
**I'm on the second row, third from right**

I remember vividly the time that David Smith and I got into a disagreement and started to scuffle. Well, Mr. Clark didn't allow any fighting at his school and he had a good way to stop it. He went into the office and brought out some boxing gloves and made each of us put on a pair. Then he said, "Now go at it." I hit David and David hit me and both our noses started bleeding. That was the end of that! David and I became best friends and finished out our years at Shepherd School without ever fighting again.

I learned a lot at good ole Shepherd School. Mrs. Ethel Hethcox was my fifth grade teacher. She was one of the most memorable teachers I had. She even let us write, direct, and act in our own play about frontier life in America. I thought that was pretty cool. Evelyn Brown and I did most of the writing as well as I remember.

**Gary Ervin, David Smith, Jimmy Johnson, and Jerry Waugh in our fifth-grade school play**

David Smith, Jerry Waugh, Jimmy Johnson, and Gary Ervin were a few of the main characters. Gary was the head Indian and he got to wear feathers and carry a bow and some arrows. The rest of us got to wear coonskin caps like Davy Crockett wore. We made gun barrels out of broomsticks, the stocks out of scrap wood, and then painted the whole thing black. The guns looked really authentic from where the audience was sitting. Everybody had a part or something to do. It was quite a production.

One particular thing really stands out in my mind about Shepherd School; and that was the "Sugar Bowl". Actually, that's what we affectionately called the septic tank area. It was located where the ground sloped in left field down to a large concrete holding tank. There was some sand below the holding tank that was scattered between concrete barriers, to absorb odors, among other things. (It didn't always work.) If someone hit a baseball all the way to the "Sugar Bowl", it was deemed a home run—no questions asked. Usually a smaller kid was unanimously elected by the bigger boys to be the one who had to climb down in that thing; and retrieve the ball. Guess who was often elected for that unpleasant task? The job didn't pay anything, either.

I was athletically challenged to a fault, but nonetheless, I still played baseball with the rest of the boys. Left field was the position I was usually relegated to play because there was not much action out there. I couldn't judge fly balls worth spit, and usually watched helplessly as they either dropped in front of me or sailed over my head.

I could hit pretty well and enjoyed my times at bat. However, the curve ball gave me a lot of trouble. Dwight Neill was a year older than I and could throw a hard curve ball. He called it his "head-hunter" pitch. It looked as if the ball was coming straight at your head, then it would suddenly break down and away from you. I was scared to bat when Dwight was pitching. I knew that he was going to throw that "head-hunter", and he knew that I was afraid of it. Dwight would throw that doggoned thing at me every time I was batting and I don't remember ever getting a single hit off him.

The Iredell County School Board voted to build a new kitchen, lunchroom, and library for our school in the mid 1950's. An entirely separate building from the main schoolhouse was erected and a covered walkway was built to join the two buildings. I didn't mind walking out in the open a little ways to go eat my lunch.

We always had great food and I could hardly wait for lunch. Believe it or not, my favorite meal at school was pinto beans and cornbread—just like we had at home. There would be large bowls of chopped, raw onions placed on each table for our indulgence. We country boys would load our plates with those raw onions and pinto beans and eat with the gusto of a hound dog. I really felt sorry for our teachers who had to endure the sounds and odors of many post-prandial indiscretions. Of course, the emanations were accidental in nature, but they had the same effect. Giggles would abound, but, admissions of guilt were very rare. The first-smeller-is-the-very-feller-rule was accepted as the law in our class.

Sometimes, for dessert, there would be ginger cake with lemon sauce, topped with a dollop of whipped cream. I never ate anything sweet that I didn't like and I became a pretty good authority on desserts. That ginger cake with lemon sauce was one of the best desserts we ever had at Shepherd School.

We could buy an extra carton of milk for three cents and I would usually buy two extra ones, because I needed them to help wash down my second plate of food. We were allowed to get second helpings as long as there was plenty of food left over. I was always hungry and took advantage of any extra food.

The library was also in the lunchroom and I enjoyed reading immensely. I couldn't wait for the library to get the latest edition of *Ideals*. It was a colorful magazine-type book filled with beautiful photographs and poems that never failed to inspire me. I vowed that someday I would visit some of the places that were often featured in the book. I also read the *State* Magazine every month and enjoyed its wonderful stories about North Carolina and its people. It was crammed full of articles that were helpful if we needed to do a project about North Carolina.

One special group of books was bound with the same royal blue bindings. They were biographies about famous Americans and I read every one of them. They were especially handy for those book reports that our teachers often required.

I even read poetry and memorized several poems. Henry Wadsworth Longfellow and Robert Frost were my favorite poets. I memorized Eugene Field's poem, *Jest 'fore Christmas*, and recited it in front of my fifth grade class.

Mama and Daddy both loved to read. Daddy had the Iredell County Bookmobile stop by our house on a regular basis. It was a portable library that allowed us to check out books for three weeks at a time. The Bookmobile provided a great service for rural Iredell County citizens. I learned how much fun reading can really be by observing the pure joy that my parents obtained from sitting down with a good book. I still read at least two books a week. I go to Mooresville's new public library practically every day.

Many of my classmates have become successful citizens and live all across the country. Some of us have stayed near Mooresville.

Gary Ervin and David Smith have since passed away, as well as several of my other classmates of the 1950-1958 Class of Shepherd School. I still see some of the gang occasionally around town. The friendships forged there have been long-lasting and I will always cherish my memories of those times spent at Shepherd School. They are some of the best memories of my life.

The venerated Shepherd School building that I remember has been torn down and a new one was built in front of it nearer the highway in 2000. I have a brick from the old school building in my collections of memorabilia. I think I'll just hang on to it—you never know when you're going to need a historic brick.

# Vacations

The Blue Ridge Mountains were only a little over an hour from where we lived. We particularly loved the Blue Ridge Parkway and went as often as we could even if it was just to ride a few miles along its scenic route on Sunday afternoons. Mama and Laura never passed up an opportunity to take someone's picture in any kind of weather. I remember that my skinny, little arms almost froze off having my picture made in front of an icy waterfall.

**Roger, Daddy, and me in front of the frozen waterfall**

At one time or another, we have traveled the entire length of the Blue Ridge Parkway from Cherokee, North Carolina all the way to Waynesboro, Virginia, where the Parkway ends. Shenandoah National Park begins there and the Parkway becomes Skyline Drive and goes all the way to Front Royal, Virginia

I am still awed by the natural beauty of the mountains when the hillsides come alive each October with the blazing colors of autumn. Spring bursts forth with its own myriad of colors and is depicted beautifully by the rhododendron and flame azaleas. Rustic cabins and split-rail fences enhance the roadside making it one of the most scenic highways in America. To me, Doughton Park in Alleghany County, North Carolina is one of the most beautiful areas on the entire five-hundred miles of the Blue Ridge Parkway. The Parkway is still my favorite road in the United States. Even today, I try to traverse its meandering route along the crest of the mountains at least once a month.

Even though we didn't have a whole lot of money, somehow Daddy and Mama would take us on some kind of extended vacation every year or two. Extended for us meant, that we got to spend at least one night somewhere away from home.

We all liked the mountains very much, so one year they took us to the Shenandoah National Park in Virginia, to ride along the Skyline Drive. Daddy would often pull over to the side of the road and let us look out across the picturesque Shenandoah Valley. It was a beautiful sight for these young eyes to behold. The broad valley looked as if someone had taken colorful swatches of cloth, sewn them together into a patchwork quilt, and flung it across the contour of the land. (Kind of sounds poetic, doesn't it?) We were all mesmerized by the entire scene that lay before us.

We spent the night near Waynesboro, Virginia at a little motor court. There was a restaurant located on the premises and Daddy took us there for breakfast about six o'clock the next morning. We didn't get to eat in a restaurant too often and that soon became very obvious. Daddy had told us in advance that we could order anything we wanted for breakfast—that in itself was a first time experience.

When the waiter approached our table and asked what we would like for breakfast, I quickly said, "I want two hot dogs, all the way." (That's slaw, mustard, chili, and onions.) I wasn't about to take the chance that Daddy would change his mind about us ordering what we wanted. When Daddy heard me order hot dogs for breakfast, I thought he would crawl under his chair.

He sat up a little straighter as the waiter moved over to where Laura was seated; after all, she was three years older. The waiter hadn't fully recovered from my order as of yet, nevertheless, while glancing over at Daddy; boldly asked Laura what she would like to have. Laura said without blinking an eye, "I want two hot dogs, all the way." I watched my Daddy turn red with embarrassment as he once again slid down in his seat.

Daddy knew without a shadow of a doubt that he could depend on his eldest son not to embarrass him by ordering two hot dogs, all the way, at six o'clock in the morning.

Daddy sat a little straighter in his seat again, this time trying to salvage a little pride in his offspring, and looked at Roger hopefully. Well, this little waiter bravely approached my big brother and asked anxiously, "Do you want two hot dogs, all the way, too?"

"No," Roger replied succinctly, "I want three hot dogs, all the way." I thought Daddy would never bounce back from that episode in humility, brought on by the issues of his marriage, but he did, and let us have our hot dogs for breakfast.

I don't think any of us kids, ever had enough hot dogs. We definitely were not going to pass up an opportunity to have some then.

Mama didn't get up for breakfast and she missed all the fun.

We didn't get to go to the Smoky Mountains very often because they were about four hours from home. But I do remember going to the Great Smoky Mountain National Park one time though and seeing a real live, wild bear. Mama wanted a picture of it, so Laura just walked right up to that bear, looked him in the eye from a distance of about ten feet, said smile, took his picture, and then ran back to the car. I don't think Laura was scared of "squat". I didn't get out of the car!

**Laura's Smoky Mountain bear**

Only one road crosses the Smoky Mountain National Park and it is extremely curvy. The road runs from Cherokee, North Carolina to Gatlinburg, Tennessee. There is a place where the road switches back so much that you go around in a circle and cross right over the same road you are on. That particular engineering marvel is called the Loop-Over and it really fascinated Mama. She even bought a postcard with a picture of the Loop-Over on it.

We never took any extensive vacations to exotic places or anything, but when we went somewhere, we thoroughly enjoyed every minute of it. I guess one of the most exotic places we visited was Maggie Valley, North Carolina where we saw a man milk a rattlesnake at The Soco Reptile Gardens. I still can't believe we did that! Why Daddy wasted good money for us to see that is beyond me.

**Laura's picture of us in the Smoky Mountains**

Cherokee was not far from Maggie Valley and we visited there while in the Smoky Mountains. Full-blooded Cherokee Indians were everywhere you turned. They even had tepees along the main street that impressed young people like me. Roger bought a corn-cob pipe in one of the many gift shops. We later used it to smoke our RJR tobacco when we were camping out. I bought myself an authentic Indian headdress, replete with brightly colored feathers. (I think the doggoned thing was made in China.) I found that Indian headdress the other day. It's upstairs in the gallery along with everything else I can't part with.

One time, we spent the night in Robbinsville, North Carolina while visiting the Smoky Mountains and Fontana Dam. We stayed in an old upstairs room over a store. The only window had a musty smelling screen on it and what little air that did come through it reeked with the smell of that awful must. Predictably, I had an acute attack of asthma. Daddy had to finally take me down to the car where my wheezing would not keep everybody else awake. I couldn't sleep because I could barely get my breath and had to sit up all night. Daddy didn't get any sleep either, so about 4:30 in the morning, he woke the rest of the family, loaded the car, and told Mama to drive.

Mama had never driven in the mountains before, particularly not in the dark. Daddy just said, "Drive woman," and Mama drove. Neither one of them were too happy about the whole situation.

Daylight finally came and Mama pulled over beside the Tennessee River. Everyone was a little disgruntled by then and a good rest was needed by all. Breathing had become easier for me during the morning, so we kids went wading in the frigid waters of the river while Mama and Daddy slept on a blanket in the shade. Everything worked out as usual and we all were happy as we went on our way. However, Mama never drove on vacation again.

Sometimes, we just went to the Brushy Mountains between Taylorsville and North Wilkesboro, North Carolina and rode around on dirt roads among the apple orchards. That was fun, too. Daddy would stop the car and let us pick up apples from the ditches along the road. He said that wasn't stealing—the apples would have gone to waste anyway. We helped a lot of orchard owners keep their ditches clean in the fall of the year. He always stopped at an apple house and bought some apples, too. Daddy was a man of principles and believed in doing what he thought was right. He thought that if we were going to pick up some of their free apples, the least we could do was to buy some, too.

Daddy always liked to travel the dirt roads that went so far back in the mountains that the sun set between where we were and the main highway. I'll have to admit that I still like doing that, too.

I honestly believe that I inherited my wanderlust from him. I'll always regret that I never had the chance to enjoy my daddy's company on rides to the mountains by ourselves. He died while I was in my mid-twenties—the age I still thought that I knew everything. I realize now, that I missed out on some wonderful memories that only a son and father can share.

Several years ago, I started going over to Uncle Tom Brantley's house every Saturday morning around 6:00 or so and visiting with him. He told me more about my daddy than I had ever known before. He and Daddy were close throughout their lives; therefore he was able to share many amusing anecdotes about their childhoods.

Uncle Tom liked to ride as much as Daddy did and I would often take him with me to the mountains. He told me one time that he thought he had seen the mountains before; but after riding along with me on some of the back roads, he realized he had never really seen them up close and personal. I took Uncle Tom to the Outer Banks, too and we really had a great trip together. We visited the water-treatment plant that he helped build in Elizabeth City, North Carolina. He even talked with one of the men who worked with him on the job. He thoroughly enjoyed getting to reminisce with his old co-worker.

I thank God for Uncle Tom. Spending time with him somewhat assuaged the guilt I felt for not sharing quality time with Daddy. Uncle Tom passed away in 2004 and I miss him greatly, too.

We really liked going to the beach, too but didn't get to go very often. We couldn't afford to stay in one of the ocean front homes and usually settled for one of the older houses a few blocks from the shore. One old house we stayed in was painted a sickly looking yellow. The window screens were so rusty and dirty that very little air made it through them. The kitchen had an old-fashioned kerosene cook stove with burners that had to be lit with a match before we could even cook. Daddy cooked fish one night that he and Roger had caught off the pier and it smoked the house up so badly that I had a severe attack of asthma and kept everybody up all night. In later years, things looked a little better financially; and we stayed in some better places. My asthma attacks were fewer, too.

**I loved those rafts**

I loved to ride the waves on the rafts that you could rent by the hour. The canvas surfaces on the rafts were extremely rough and they would always rub my nipples raw, but I rode the rafts anyway.

Daddy usually got Roger and me up before daylight to go swimming in the ocean. The water would be warmer than the air and the porpoise would swim within ten or twelve feet of us. All that swimming would give me a heck of an appetite. I would eat five or six eggs and a half of a loaf of bread when we got back to the house. I still couldn't gain any weight because of my asthma. I was so skinny then that I had to stand with somebody just to get my picture taken. Laura seemed to be the one who took a lot of our pictures. Roger had given Mama a little Kodak Brownie camera one year for Christmas and most of the pictures in this book were taken with that little camera. It did a pretty good job of capturing our lives for posterity.

**Mama, Daddy, and me at the beach**

I remember our family going to White Lake, near Elizabethtown, North Carolina only one time. I will never forget its crystal clear waters. You could see the bottom of the lake just as clearly if you were in ten feet of water or in only two feet. I dove off the dock as soon as we got there and scraped my "noggin" on the bottom. I thought the water was a lot deeper than it was—the clarity of the water made it difficult to judge the depth.

I don't remember exactly where we stayed, but there was a boat moored beside the dock. I wanted to have my picture made sitting on it to impress the girls when I got back home. They probably knew that I never rode in the boat anyway, but it was the thought that counted.

**Posing at White Lake**

Everywhere our parents took us was an adventure in itself. We saw a lot and we did a lot, but it was all on a tight budget. I think the only time we really splurged was in Waynesboro, Virginia, when Daddy had to buy all those hot dogs.

# Indoor Plumbing

Daddy built a wall between the kitchen and our little breakfast nook. Then, he made a new doorway from the back porch into our newly built bathroom. We were going to be what you called "uptown", and we weren't going to have to run to the little outhouse in the backyard anymore. We were even going to have a commode. However, there wasn't going to be any heat in the bathroom—the Ketchies hadn't climbed that far up the social ladder quite yet.

The moment had arrived for the tub to be installed, and I could hardly wait. As I was told, this would be the largest fixture in the entire house. I was only about five or six years old at the time and this was a major event. The heavy, cast iron tub was finally maneuvered into position, and I couldn't get over the funny looking claw feet that held up the tub. But the crowning moment was when they fastened the spigots to the front of it. It was a combination mechanism that had a knob for hot and a knob for cold. The contraption came down a little ways and was joined in the middle so that the hot and cold water could mix together. It had this extremely odd looking spout with weird rings around it. I thought that this was the funniest looking thing I had ever seen. I started laughing and couldn't stop. I laughed so hard and so long over the silly looking thing sticking out of the front of our bathtub that I started wetting my pants and I couldn't stop. I believe I was the first one to take advantage of our new tub. Mama had to give me a bath immediately due to my inability to control my enthusiasm.

I had no idea how the upper crust of society lived, but with this indoor bathroom, I was getting a pretty good handle on it. Like I said before, there was no heat in the new bathroom; so Daddy brought in an old kerosene heater to make it more comfortable in the winter. That heater was like having a little bit of Heaven right in the room with us. Mother would take me out of the tub and dry off my little tail in front of that heater, just like I thought the rich folks did. Daddy built a cabinet into the back wall of the bathroom so Mama would have a place to store medicine and that nasty Milk of Magnesia. We had finally arrived!

One day, Daddy decided, or Mama suggested pretty strongly, that we needed a basement under the house. As I found out later, that's where they usually put basements. Most of the time, Mama could convince Daddy to do just about anything; so the monumental undertaking of building the Ketchie's basement began.

Daddy and Roger crawled under the house and started shoveling the dirt with a couple of short-handled shovels. They would put the dirt into five-gallon buckets and then carry them out from under the house. This was a slow and tedious task. I remembered helping some, but I was sure glad that I was too young to do too much of that stuff called manual labor. I had heard about manual labor and wasn't too thrilled about the whole concept. Daddy finally brought Uncle Gordon's mule, Bill, to the house, with a strange looking contraption hooked behind him. I remember Daddy calling it a drag-pan. Well, he and Roger would drag that thing under the house and fill it with dirt. Then Daddy would have to crawl out from under the house and get Old Bill to drag the pan all the way into the backyard where they would dump the dirt out of it. This process was repeated over and over until I got tired of watching them. I decided that my valuable time could be better spent playing in the fresh pile of dirt that had appeared in our backyard.

Mama became disgruntled very easily. I think this basement project was getting a little out of hand, and I wasn't making her very happy, either, by playing in the big pile of red dirt. How was I to know that you couldn't get that stuff out of your clothes? I was used to playing with my cars and trucks on level ground in the sand, and this huge pile of red dirt added another dimension to my play. I now had mountains!

After a sufficient amount of dirt had been excavated from under the house, Daddy commenced to laying cinder blocks for the walls. Then a concrete floor was poured.

There was no way to enter the basement from inside the house; so Daddy made some steps out of cinder blocks and built a covered entrance with a short, wooden door that led to the basement from outside. He then laid a brick walkway to the back door of our house to finish the project.

There was a small place above the basement door where Roger would hide his secret stuff from me—including his cigarettes. I knew he hid his stuff there but I never told anyone about it because I didn't want to get him into trouble; he was a good big brother.

**Basement entrance behind Laura and Larry**

Daddy took showers while in the Army and found that he liked them better than tub baths. I didn't particularly like either one. He ran some water pipes from the bathroom upstairs to the basement and installed the first shower in the Ketchie household. We were so proud we didn't know how to act. Daddy dug a hole in the floor of the basement and installed a drain for the shower, and we were in business.

I didn't know much about modesty, yet; so Roger and I, in order to save time and hot water, were often required to take our showers at the same time. One evening, we were soaped up really well when I looked up and saw a huge blacksnake crawling along the ledge where we kept the soap. Seeing the snake caused me to employ my usual specialized mode of alerting someone of imminent danger. (I started screaming my head off). Then Roger saw the snake and calmly, considering the circumstances, took a towel and ran the slithering serpent into a hole that had been drilled through a floor sill on the outside wall. I was afraid to finish my shower, but Roger convinced me that it was the thing to do. I don't think he was too wild about seeing his skinny, little, brother running naked around the back of the house.

Daddy nailed an old Mason jar lid over the hole and assured me that this had been a one-time occurrence and that I should continue to take my showers in the basement. What choice did I have?

We moved our old Apex washing machine with rubber ringers into the basement and placed it beside twin tubs that were made especially to use while washing clothes. One of the tubs was for the first rinse, once the clothes had been brought out of the washing machine and run through the ringer. The second tub was for the final rinse. We had to place the ringer over the tubs so the clothes could pass from one to another.

Wash day was a big event at our house. All of us kids got to take turns draining the washing machine and the tubs. (Sometimes I think I can still smell that wash-water.)

The water had to be drained into foot tubs, carried up the stairs, and then dumped on Mama's hydrangeas. The lucky one that drained the tubs and washing machine got to keep all the money they found at the bottom of them. I think Daddy, at times, left a little change in his pockets on purpose so we could find a dime or two. Like I've always said, he was a good daddy.

The wash was then hung along the clotheslines that Daddy had strung between two tall, chestnut oak trees in the backyard. I remember helping Laura hang clothes one day, when something purple splattered on my arm. I thought Roger was hiding and throwing pokeberries at us. The thought of him doing that to us made me madder with each passing minute. I began yelling at him to show himself, so I could throw a big, hard chestnut acorn at him, but he never answered my challenge. I soon realized that it was just a bird dropping his colorful load on me. Pokeberries were ripe and plentiful, and birds loved to eat them. I didn't think about birds using them as ammunition, too. That's the way my luck usually ran. I couldn't blame anything on Roger this time.

The best thing about the basement for us kids was that it never drained well. I think all the rainwater that fell at Mr. Blackwelder's house naturally gravitated across the driveway and ended up under our house. After a big rain, the cold, dirty, brown water would be up to my waist in our basement. It was almost like we had our very own indoor pool. We weren't proud; we would swim in whatever the good Lord provided. Daddy finally had to install a sump-pump into the basement floor because our indoor swimming pool kept getting deeper with each rain. That ended the reign of the Ketchie's indoor swimming pool

We Ketchies were living on the cutting edge of technology. We now had our own indoor plumbing. After all, Daddy read *Popular Mechanics*

The outhouse was no longer needed, so Roger and I had the prestigious honor of pushing it over. Daddy filled in the big hole that was left, and all was well with the world at the Ketchie house on Statesville Highway.

# Rat Killing

You have never had real fun until you've participated in a "rat killing". We had a hog pen that was situated behind our house, and Mama saw to it that it was at the <u>very</u> back of our one-acre lot. She didn't care for the noise or the smell. Daddy built a house, of sorts, for the hogs that rested on a concrete slab. The feeding trough ran along the edge of the fence beneath a shady, chestnut oak tree. Laura fell into the trough one day while we were feeding the hogs, and Bill Overcash never let her forget that incident.

The hogs had a fairly good-sized lot in which to roam and wallow. We would fill some of their favorite wallowing spots with water and watch them roll around in the mud.

Beneath the concrete slab where the hogs lived were numerous holes and tunnels where rats ran wild. Those blasted varmints were eating the hog feed like it was candy or *Purina Rat Chow*. It was getting to the point where they were acting like they owned the place. There must have been twenty or thirty of them. We tried drowning them by running a water hose under the slab, but it didn't do any good. I think they liked it! We seemed to be fighting a losing battle with the rat population.

Daddy taught Roger and me to shoot a .22 caliber rifle while we were still pretty young. Daddy was a crack shot—whatever that means. We would throw coins or chinaberries in the air, and he could shoot them with his Remington pump rifle before they even thought about coming down. Roger and I could shoot those little chinaberries off the tree if the wind wasn't blowing. We could shoot cans while they were in the air, but that wasn't like shooting coins. In our eyes, Daddy was a regular Buffalo Bill.

On a slow day when Daddy didn't have anything for us to do, Roger and I would take our rifles out to the hog lot, sit on an old bucket, and wait for a big, fat rat to make his appearance. Pretty soon, one would poke his head out from under the concrete slab. Roger was always good to me and would let me take the first shot. I was cautioned to wait until the rat was completely out of the hole before shooting. If I shot him when he was just coming out of the hole, he would block the entrance and others wouldn't be able to get out, and we didn't want that. We wanted to get as many as we could.

Daddy kept the hog feed in a big barrel in the car shed (that's "garage" to city folks). We were required to add a couple of big scoops of it to the slop before we carried it to the hogs. Rats just loved that sweet smelling, hog feed. I always saw one or two of them near the barrel every time I went to slop the hogs.

They acted like they owned the car shed, too. Frankly, it was getting a little old, seeing those rascals looking up at me and almost daring me to do something.

Sometimes we could hear Mama scream when she was getting in the car. She finally begged us to get rid of those filthy rats. That's how "rat killing" evolved into such a serious job for us boys. We would kill several in a day, but there just seemed to be an endless supply of them. We weren't mean or anything; we were just country boys providing a service. I know, shooting defenseless rats sounds cruel, but it was a necessary job. Those rats carried diseases, ate our hogs' food and terrorized our mother.

One time, Daddy made some miniature hollows to catch small animals. They worked just exactly like our rabbit hollows—they were just built on a smaller scale. One summer day, I came up with the brilliant idea of catching a big, rat in one of those little hollows. I was going to be a regular "Jungle Jim" and capture wild animals alive.

I went to the garage, took a little hog feed out of the barrel, and made a trail about three or four feet long with it. The trail ended just a little inside the entrance of one of the hollows. Then, I made me a seat by propping up an old, Golden Crust breadbox on the dirt floor of the garage to watch this historical event unfold. I wasn't there five minutes before one of those nasty long-tailed menaces made his appearance. Sure enough, that rat stuck his nose out from under the feed barrel and started sniffing away at the tempting trail of feed. He would sniff and stretch as far as he could, while keeping his back legs safely under the barrel. This went on for awhile, and all of a sudden, his back legs would catch up with the rest of him. Then he would slowly make his way up the trail to the hollow. I didn't think he would ever go in it, but he finally did, and the door flew down with great authority. I had caught a big one, too; and I was excited.

I picked up the rat-filled hollow and ran to Grandma's house as fast as my little legs could carry me. I didn't know what I was going to do with a live rat, but I was sure Grandma would know exactly what to do with this thieving rodent.

As per Grandma's instructions, I proceeded toward the barn and was immediately followed by a whole clowder of cats. I didn't even make it to the barn before I stopped and started repeating, "Here kitty, kitty, here kitty, kitty". Man, before long, I had a captive audience. I never figured out how they knew what I was carrying. Anyway, I knelt down and very slowly lifted the door to the rat hollow. Well, that rascal took off like a shot toward the barn. He didn't make it to within twenty feet of his intended destination before one of Grandma's calico cats brought him down—she took him home with her for supper.

I went back to our car shed and caught five or six more of those hog-feed-stealing rats and made a lot more of Grandma's cats extremely happy. They even began waiting for me expectantly. I guess I became somewhat of a folk hero to the entire feline community at Grandma's farm.

I thought those rats must be as dumb as a bag of hammers because I kept on catching them the same old way all day long. I tired of this sport later in the evening and thought I would try something a little different. I decided to make a trail of the hog feed all the way up to the Golden Crust breadbox on which I was sitting. I thought it would be kind of interesting if the trail led right up to my bare, big toe.

I had just gotten settled on my breadbox when one of the biggest rats I had ever seen began sniffing his way out from under the feed barrel. I was going to wait him out and see if he would come all the way to my foot. That bugger came sniffing right toward my big toe, but I was determined not to move. I was going to see how close he would come to me before he backed off and ran for cover. Well, that rascal crept slowly and cautiously until he was about twelve inches from my right foot. Then, all of a sudden, he made a dash for my big toe. That unexpected dash for some little-boy-big-toe-meat scared me so much I fell off the box. All that noise scared the rat so badly that he lost his footing before he could put on his brakes. He turned a few flips and rolled over on the ground in shock. Then, we both jumped up and he took off for parts unknown and I took off for the house. That was the last time I ever saw that rat, and that was the last time I ever did something that stupid involving wild animals.

Mr. Lackey's trash gully was another hangout for us "rat-killing aficionados". His gully was widely known for having a veritable plethora of the pestilent pests. We would often hike over to Mr. Lackey's trash dump that was located off Highway 21. It was just a good mile or so through the woods. (That was just a warm-up for a country boy.) Roger, David Wilson, and I would go to the trash gully often, just to thin the rat population down a little bit. We were really conscientious young men and only wanted to do the public a good service. I would carry my little, .22 caliber, bolt action, Springfield rifle with me and David and Roger were always packing their powerful, 12 gauge shotguns. They didn't believe in giving a rat a fighting chance. After Roger and

David started shooting those loud cannons they carried, the rats would become quite scarce. I didn't blame the rats one bit. I had always been scared to death of really loud noises, but I always wanted to be included in Roger's adventures, so there I was, with my fingers jammed in my ears.

I think that my aversion to loud noises stemmed from the Iredell County Fair and the fireworks show that they put on for us fair-goers every year. I remember screaming my head off when the big boomers exploded and shook the whole ground. I could feel my heart pounding inside my chest and would hold onto Mama for dear life. I was probably five or six years old at the time this life-altering event took place. I still don't like extremely loud noises!

Well, David and Roger were quite proficient in the use of their shotguns. Sometimes I, because of my youth and inexperience, would be requested to throw tin cans into the air as I stood between the two marksmen. One would blast the can as it reached its zenith, and the can would be knocked toward the other one. These boys were really good shots. They would shoot that old can back and forth toward each other until they emptied their guns. All this would take place while I was holding my ears.

One time, instead of a can, Roger tossed an old jar to me that was half-filled with a milky-looking liquid. Without thinking, I threw it up as high as I could, and they both shot it at the same time. Foul, rotten, slimy, mayonnaise came raining down on my little white head—not to mention the broken glass. I had been had again!

Mr. Lackey's gully was not only good for "rat killing", but provided a source of entertainment for us country folks. He collected trash from the people who lived out in the country and brought it to his gully for its final resting place. The trash never got much rest when we were around, though. We enjoyed rummaging through the trash and finding all kinds of neat stuff.

Sometimes in the winter, when the snakes were hibernating, Daddy's sisters, Sarah, Ruth, and Catherine and

I would often go "trash-piling" together and find lots of discarded treasures. Once, Aunt Sarah found $22 stuffed inside an old pocketbook. She thought she had died and gone to Heaven. If there had been any identification anywhere in the purse, she would have sought out the owner and returned the money. Aunt Sarah evidently needed the money more than the previous owner, because there was no identification to be found. Many of the glass jars we used for canning came from the trash gully. Sometimes we would find more loot than we could carry in one trip. We would traipse all the way home and unload so we could go back again. The long walk was worth it! We really enjoyed our times together on these treasure hunts. One time, Daddy found a Bulova watch that kept surprisingly accurate time. He wore that watch until he passed away.

We never knew what we would encounter on one of our excursions to the trash pile. Sometimes, it would be a hidden treasure. Sometimes it would be a bunch of rats that needed to be called home to that big trash pile in the sky. We did our best to hasten their journey on the road to glory.

# Earning Spending Money

I realized, as I grew older, that having some money to rattle around in my pocket provided me with a sense of well-being. I may have gotten a small allowance when I was young, but if I did, I don't remember it. We had chores to do, and were expected to do them, as our contribution to the Ketchie household. We didn't give it very much thought. That's just the way it was.

Roger and I often read the ads in magazines that promised riches if we only sold enough greeting cards, or packets of seeds. We, being the financially challenged young boys that we were, hastily sent off for the opportunity to earn riches untold. It never worked out quite that well.

Roger was a bit shy and didn't like going around the neighborhood, knocking on doors, and making a nuisance out of himself, so I being his loquacious little brother with the winning smile; was usually left to sell most of our newly acquired merchandise.

I could always depend on Mrs. R.C. Millsaps to be unable to say "no" to the marvelous products that I brought right to her door. It must have been my hundred-watt smile that weakened her resistance, because she always bought some greeting cards or a few packets of garden seeds. I remember thinking—she surely uses a lot of cards and seeds—she's bought a ton of them over the years.

I was informed after the passing of Mrs. Millsaps, that her children found a cabinet crammed full of packages of seeds and unused boxes of greeting cards. She was forevermore, one sweet lady and I will always be grateful for her kindness, and her giving this one little country boy a leg up in the world of commerce.

Mrs. "Carby" Honeycutt lived directly across the road from Mrs. Millsaps and I would always call on her, too. I did not discriminate; I gave her the same fabulous opportunity to purchase some of those beautiful greeting cards, too. I explained to my customers how convenient it would be to have the cards on hand and ready to use, when needed. It was extremely difficult for them to resist that kind of logic.

I also expected my own family to make a purchase; and Mama was usually a soft touch to her youngest offspring's entreaties. My great-aunt, Lil Patten, and her daughter Lillian, would often buy a dollar box of greeting cards. The seeds sold for only ten cents a pack, and making much money off of them was slow-going.

Roger and I would do odd jobs around the neighborhood that would often add a dollar or two to our pockets. We occasionally cleaned out the goldfish ponds for Aunt Lil Patten, Aunt Ella Ketchie, and Mildred Chandler. I never understood why there were so many goldfish ponds in our neighborhood. It might just have been a Ketchie thing, I don't know. I did know that neither, Grandma or our family ever had the money to build a goldfish pond in our yards. Besides not having the money—it was totally out of our character and a little above our raising. Nevertheless, the ponds provided a way for us to make some money. Each of those goldfish pond owners was related to us, but even so, they still needed help with the difficult task of cleaning and draining their ponds.

We also cleaned out Aunt Lil's gutters. We didn't know anyone else that even owned gutters, so this was a specialized job. It was also dangerous for us kids to scramble around on the roof of her house without falling off, so this hazardous undertaking paid a little more.

Mr. Lon and Mrs. Peggy Malcolm had lived next door to us for years, but around 1958, moved up the road and across from Carl Harkey's store. Their new digs had an old rusty, tin roof that looked really bad.

One hot July day, I was in an entrepreneurial mood, and asked Mr. Malcolm if he would like to have his roof painted with aluminum paint so it would reflect the scorching summer sun. He thought it might be a good idea and bought the paint so I could begin the arduous task.

Folks, a tin roof in the month of July is hot, and don't let anyone try to tell you anything differently. It is also difficult to find a really comfortable position in which to paint a roof that slants very much. I finally decided to make an executive decision, since I was the only one there, and just slid along on my skinny little butt while I slapped that aluminum paint across the rows and rows of hot tin. Well, sliding along on my skinny little butt worked fairly well for the first few hours, but the last few hours wore some really nasty blisters in places that normally wouldn't have any.

By the way, aluminum paint really does reflect the scorching summer sun. I didn't know too much about science, so I thought it would be cooler if I only wore a pair of shorts and no shirt. Well, when I finished the job, I was about as red as a beet and hurt all over my body. My exposed skin was blistered so badly that it peeled off in huge layers.

To make matters worse, I don't think I thought the painting project through like I should have. My biggest mistake was not agreeing with Mr. Malcolm on a price for this onerous undertaking. I just asked him to pay me what he thought the two-day job was worth.

Mr. Malcolm was really pleased with the way his shiny roof now looked and he thought the job was worth about fifteen dollars. I thought that my blisters alone were worth more in the neighborhood of fifty dollars. I guess it must have been the generation gap or something because he thought he was being generous.

Mr. Malcolm said that he would recommend me for roof-painting to anyone who was interested in having theirs done. I informed him that I was retiring from the roof painting business and was going to concentrate all my energies toward cotton picking. (I hated cotton picking worse, but I didn't tell him that little fact.)

225

I had always helped on the farm during harvest time and Uncle Gordon would sometimes pay me. Well let me tell you right now, payment was definitely required if this little, white-headed boy picked any cotton. That was one job that I did not like at all and I was not about to pick cotton for free. If I had known the word, "loathe", when I was young, I would have used it then, to describe my feelings pertaining to cotton picking. My back still hurts from bending over all day in the cotton patch, fifty years ago. If someone even mentions cotton picking, I get a twinge of pain in my lower back.

**The bane of my existence—the cotton patch**

I never understood how in the world Aunt Lib, Aunt Ruth, and Aunt Catherine could pick four-hundred pounds of cotton a day. I don't mean collectively, I mean, EACH! It was all I could do to pick a hundred pounds. One time, I picked a little over a hundred and fifty pounds and got one-and-a-half cents a pound for my labor. Aunt Lib's brother, Neel Morrow, offered me two cents a pound to pick for him at his patch in Amity Hill. If I picked really hard I could make close to three dollars a day working for Neel. It was kind of like a raise, I guess you could say.

I picked cotton for Grandma Ketchie, Uncle Gene Rogers, and Neel Morrow. I didn't want to spread my cotton-picking prowess around too much and have every farmer in the neighborhood wanting me to come to their aid.

I thought that the entire world was out to get me when I was young. They even let us out of school early during cotton picking season so we could have more daylight to work longer. I don't know who came up with that idea, but it was not very popular among us cotton-picking students. For those who didn't have to pick, it was a real treat.

I always stopped by Grandma's big pear tree on the way to the patch and picked a pear or two just so I would have a little something to tide me over until supper. I remember the only thing that helped me to get from one end of a row to the other was the jar of water waiting at the other end. Sometimes, Aunt Lib would make some homemade lemonade and bring it to the patch in a gallon jar. We would cover the jar with a sack to keep the relentless sun from getting it too hot. I might be exaggerating a little bit, but I believe Aunt Lib's cool lemonade saved my life more than once.

The dad-blamed cotton bolls had sharp burrs that projected past the soft cotton; and when you reached to get the cotton, the blasted things would tear into your fingers and would have them bleeding after only a couple of rows. I was just too tender, I guess. Daddy always said that I was a lot like my Mama. Come to think of it, I never saw my mama pick any cotton.

I found out that there was a lot of different ways to make money besides working on the farm. I often pumped gas at Carl Harkey's store, but usually got paid in watermelons or something else to eat. That suited me just fine—that was what I was going to spend my money on anyway.

I also had a part-time job delivering newspapers for the Statesville Record and Landmark. Mr. Alvah Miller picked me up at Carl Harkey's store and then drove us to Statesville to the back of the Record and Landmark building to get the newspapers everyday. Most of them had to be rolled and fastened with rubber bands in the thirty minutes it took to drive back to Mooresville.

We then delivered them all over Mooresville and the surrounding area, throwing neatly wrapped newspapers into customer's yards. I always threw mine as far as I could so the customer wouldn't have to walk very far to get it. Sometimes, I could throw it across their lawns and onto their porches. The customers really liked that!

Mr. Miller often made me do the collecting, too. I didn't like that job at all. More often than you would imagine, I was informed by the customer that they couldn't pay their paper bill for that month. I never knew what to do when that happened, but I didn't want to have to get the Mafia after them, so I just told Mr. Miller, and he handled it.

I went to work at City Grocery and Market on Main Street in Mooresville when I was in the tenth grade. John Alec McLean owned the store and was one of the finest men I have ever known. He taught me so much about customer service, how to buy produce, cut up a chicken, and still have fun while working. I had never had a structured job before— it was all new to me, but John was a patient man and I worked there all through high school.

I remember my first day on the job at City Grocery like it just happened last week. John Templeton managed the front part of the store and John McLean ran the meat market. No one told me how much money I was going to make, so I just asked John Templeton to keep a tab of the drinks and snacks I consumed while working and we could settle up at the end of the day. I soon discovered that delivering groceries was awful thirsty work and it also made me hungry. Well, it turned out; I owed City Grocery and Market over two dollars at the end of my first day! I was informed that I had eaten nine packs of cheese crackers, two candy bars, downed eight RCs and two Cheerwines. I failed to see much humor in the situation, but everybody else thought it was quite hilarious. It was a good thing John Alec fixed me a couple of sandwiches for lunch, or I probably would have starved to death.

After working at the grocery store for a few weeks, I began going to the Mooresville Ice Cream plant on Broad Street during my lunch hour to watch them make Drumsticks They would take a large tray filled with thirty-six waffle cones topped with vanilla ice cream, dip them upside down into a big pot of melted chocolate, and then swirl the tops of them into a tray of crumbled peanuts.

H.D. Moose would sometimes take one of the cones out of the tray and personally make me an over-sized Drumstick to eat while I watched. He would double-dip it into the chocolate and then double-roll it in the peanuts until that Drumstick probably weighed over a pound. It would take me the rest of my lunch hour just to eat it. There's nothing in the world quite like having your own personally, hand-made Drumstick!

I found that after eating one of those humongous, one-pound marvels or a double cone of their wonderful Deluxe Black Cherry ice cream, that I could make it through the rest of the afternoon on only two packs of Lance Cheese Crackers and two RCs. Just being a teenager made me hungry!

Jerry Templeton, John Templeton's son, drove the panel-truck loaded with groceries and I helped him deliver them all over Mooresville and the surrounding area.

Jerry and I also sat beside each other in Mrs. Libby Lowder's typing class at Mooresville Senior High School. Sitting us together was a mistake in judgment on her part. We were often late for work after school because of this seating arrangement. It was a law, personally written and enforced by Mrs. Lowder, that your typewriter carriage had to be centered and the cover placed neatly over your machine before class was dismissed. I would always have mine in perfect position and ready to get out of there; when Jerry would reach over and hit my return key. That would make the carriage fly out of the center position and ring the bell on the typewriter. Mrs. Lowder was never amused at this oft repeated infraction. We would have to stay after school and that made us late for work. John wasn't pleased by our tardiness, but he was a kind and patient man, and I think he felt sorry for young men who experienced mental lapses.

It was hard work, loading the groceries in big, wire baskets; and arranging them in the truck so that they would be in the right order as we made our deliveries. I think John Templeton liked to see how much stuff he could load into each one of the baskets just so he could see me struggle as I tried to carry one in each hand. He would often place twenty-four cokes, a big sack of flour, and some canned vegetables into one basket. He always said that carrying those baskets would help me become a man. I don't think it worked—it just wore me slap out!

A lot of our customers left their doors unlocked so that we could go right into their homes, put the perishables in the refrigerators, and leave the rest of the groceries on their kitchen table. It was really a good service that we provided and was appreciated by our many customers who had no transportation. We were a trustworthy bunch at City Grocery and Market.

We had lots of fun and interaction with our customers, too. There were countless regulars who lived within walking distance of the store and visited every day. Sometimes they just wanted a place to hang out and see their friends.

Frankie Owens, who was a couple of years younger than I, found much enjoyment in opening the front door of City Grocery, shooting John Templeton with his water gun, laughing, and then high-tailing it out before John could catch him. One day, John filled a twelve-quart bucket with water, set it at the front counter, and was ready for Frankie. When Frankie came through the door that day shooting his water pistol, John picked up the bucket and threw the entire twelve quarts of water all over him. I think Frankie got his just reward and that put an end to the water pistol shooting, at

City Grocery and Market. Frankie became a captain with the Mooresville Police Department and was later elected to the town board. Most people today just call him Frank, but after nearly fifty years, I still call him "Water Boy".

I went to work full-time at City Grocery around 1964 or 1965. It was a wonderful place to work and a popular place to visit while downtown, but sadly, a large number of customers charged their groceries and never paid their bills. John eventually closed the store and the town of Mooresville lost one of its finest institutions.

Between delivering newspapers and groceries, I knew just about everybody in Mooresville. It gave me a nice feeling to be able go up and down the street and always feel at home. The big drawback was, that everybody knew who's boy I was. I had to really watch what I did and not get into trouble, or Daddy would find out about it before I could get home. I wouldn't even have time to conjure up a good story.

I feel extremely fortunate to have had some kind of job since I was nine or ten years old. I not only had change in my pocket, but I learned good work habits, and got to know many citizens of my community.

# Our First Cars

Roger bought his first car from Fred Woods who worked at Mooresville Oil Company. Roger would see Fred's 1948 Ford every time we went to see Uncle Otis and Aunt Marie Honeycutt. Their driveway went right past the oil company, and he would see it parked there with a big, for sale sign on it. It got to be just too much for poor Roger to resist. The Ford was gray, with four doors, and white-wall tires. Roger bought that car for two hundred dollars. That was a lot of money back then.

It had a radio in it, but it didn't have an antenna. The only way we could listen to it was to drive the car under our clothesline and run a piece of wire to the radio. The radio worked pretty well then, but we were severely limited with our airtime, especially when Mama wanted to hang clothes to dry. I have often heard someone say, "A poor man has poor ways"—that was the truth in Roger's case.

However, we could pick up WCKY in Cincinnati, Ohio and KDKA in Pittsburgh, Pennsylvania at night—when we had it hooked up to the clothesline. The only station we could pick up around home was WHIP in Mooresville. It was just a mile down the road, toward town.

One night, Roger took David Wilson and me for a ride in his newly acquired Ford and as usual, I was relegated to the back seat. He decided to see how fast he could go while crossing the overhead bridge near Aunt Junie Oliphant's house. This bridge had a great big hump in the middle of it because it spanned the railroad tracks. Heading north, the road ended abruptly immediately after crossing the bridge. That was the direction we were headed while doing about fifty-five or sixty miles per hour. Roger and David had something to hold on to as we made the valiant jump—I didn't!

When we got airborne, my head hit the ceiling of that old Ford so hard that I heard bells ringing and I thought it popped my neck. Maybe that is what's wrong with me today.

It was a learning experience for all of us aboard that flying Ford. That's the night we discovered that brakes don't work well while in the air. When we came down and hit the pavement, we were almost in the ditch on the other side of Mazeppa Road. Once again, God watched over his careless flock by night. I don't ever remember Roger trying that stunt again. He was a pretty sharp boy.

The rear doors opened backwards on that '48 Ford and Charles Nantz would open them while we were riding down the road. (He liked to show off!) We soon found out that this action would jerk the door out of his hand and warp the hinges. Charles also would roll the window down, reach up and grab the edge of the car roof and start pulling down and pushing up on it real fast to get that top-heavy car of Roger's rocking. It was quite an unusual sight to see a 1948, four-door Ford rocking from side to side, while it was going down the road. All in all it was a good car and served Roger well.

Roger's station in the economic world improved while working with Uncle Otis in the field of construction. He always liked building things, and this job seemed to suit him well. He saved a little more money and decided to trade up in the automobile ownership department. He bought a really sharp, blue, 1953 Ford. I guess he just liked Fords. He put some fender skirts on that thing, and we were riding in high style. That was the newest automobile ever to be in our family, and I was proud to ride in it.

One night while possum hunting at Larry and Dwight Neill's; Roger turned too sharply and scraped David Wilson's bumper with the side of his newly bought Ford. It made quite an unsightly scratch all the way down the length of the car. Roger fell <u>out</u> of love with his car after that.

He traded that beautiful Ford with the unsightly scratch to "Bub" Rinehardt for a 1941 Chevrolet. We were going backwards here, folks. This was not a popular move with his little, white-headed brother. I had become accustomed to riding in a nice car when I was in his company. I didn't know exactly what Roger was thinking. This was the first time I had ever heard of anyone doing this "trading down stuff". I had a heap of trouble sorting this concept out in my mind.

**Jimmy Wilson, his 1955 Chevrolet, with Roger and his 1953 Ford.
Two cool dudes!**

Well, the first thing we had to do with that old Chevrolet was to remove the headliner that was hanging down in our faces. He never replaced the headliner and it got really hot inside that car in the summertime. The very first week, Roger had a total of four flat tires and one broken axle on that poor Chevrolet. That may not be a record; but by golly, I'll bet you it was close.

Folks, it just got worse! Roger finally drove that thing up on some blocks in the backyard, and he and Jimmy Wilson started overhauling it. They worked on it for what seemed like weeks, and the motor still sounded like it was carrying around a sack of hammers in it. You could hear that Chevrolet knocking when Roger was coming down Statesville Highway. He finally gave up, took the tires off of it, and sold the car to the Christenberry brothers for junk. He got a sum total of twenty-three dollars for his 1941 Chevrolet, and he had just spent over forty dollars for parts. It was a good thing the boy had money.

Roger continued buying and selling and losing and winning in his car deals. He acquired a 1954 Ford and had it painted black. It looked really nice with the custom fender skirts and everything. I got a little of my pride back while riding around in that one.

He ended up trading cars several more times and had a couple more Chevrolets, too. All of the Chevys' were the "Fast Back" models. Before it was all over, Roger bought a 1951 Ford pickup truck from Alex Honeycutt. He immediately had it painted red, and that is the way it stayed. It was a great truck, and Roger sold it to Daddy when he went into the Army. Daddy drove that old truck for years and had a good time owning it. Laura married Larry Neill and built a house north of Shepherds near the end of Barfield Road. There were some pinewoods beside their house, and this is where the old red truck spent its retirement.

So ends the saga of *The Cars of Roger Ketchie*. The cars he bought after he got out of the Army are another story and they have nothing to do with the automobiles that were acquired during his youth. Those first cars are the ones that will live forever in <u>my</u> memory.

David Wilson's first car was a 1949 Ford, and it was a little worse for wear. The passenger door was held shut with twine string, or baling wire. Whoever was riding shotgun had to climb out of the window or slide all the way over to the driver's side to get out of the car. David later traded up to a '51 Chevrolet "Fast Back". It had one of those backs that slanted all the way down to the rear bumper. It was pretty cool looking, with its fender skirts and all the trimmings. The big thing in the '50's was to have loud mufflers on your car. None of us had any money for those loud, glass-packed mufflers; so Roger cut some pieces of bicycle inner tubes and fitted them over the tail pipes. They made an interesting sound as they flapped back and forth, but I don't think they were such a big hit. They didn't even catch on around the Shepherd's community.

**Laura and David Wilson and his 1951 Chevy**

David's brother, Jimmy, bought a cool looking, blue, 1955 Chevrolet. One Sunday afternoon; Jimmy, Roger, and I were riding around looking at the snow covered countryside in Jimmy's car. We came to the bottom of the hill on Parkertown Road and could go no farther. The road was covered in snow and ice. We tried kicking some ruts in the surface of the frozen snow with our shoes. We even tried making ersatz chains by tying twine string around the tires, but nothing worked on Jimmy's slick tires. A kind man in a dilapidated pickup truck came to our rescue about dark and pulled us to the top of the hill. I was awful hungry by then and was glad to be delivered from my brush with starvation. (Two hours without food was about my limit.)

Charles Nantz made a car—of sorts—for himself. I think it started out as an old Ford. The roof had been cut off, and it didn't have any doors. It did have the first seat belt that I had ever seen. This unique safety device was made out of an old razor strop. Charles thought he was safe when he had that thing strapped across his lap.

This creation was his idea of a race car. His Uncle Homer raced a little bit in Hickory and one time at the Charlotte Motor Speedway. I think "racing" got into Charles' blood. (He always lived in the fast lane.)

He was the only one of our friends that owned a motorcycle. Charles was really proud of his Harley Davidson. Sometimes I rode with him on the back of that thing but I was always a little afraid. Charles was killed while riding his motorcycle less than a mile from our house. He had just graduated from Mooresville Senior High School about a week before the tragic accident.

Larry Neill, another one of our friends, drove a sporty, 1953 Mercury. It was really a neat car. Then later, he outclassed all the rest of the guys when he drove up to our house in a gorgeous, two-toned, 1956 Mercury hard top. That was about the classiest car I had ever seen in all my young life.

**Laura with Larry Neill's 1956 Mercury**

Larry and Laura started dating and soon got married while she was still in high school. That car must have done the trick.

I was too young to drive but still got to enjoy the fruits of all of the other guys' labor. They were each about eighteen years old when this car buying period in their lives began. I was only twelve or thirteen at the time and felt very privileged to be included in so much of the action.

Dwight Neill, Larry's younger brother, was a year older than I. He started driving about a year and a half before I did. He had an old, four-door, 1950 Ford that we named the "Gray Ghost". Dwight would let me drive that old Ford up and down the dirt road they lived on until I got the hang of changing the gears. The gearshift was on the column, and I had a lot trouble shifting gears, pushing in on the clutch and chewing bubble gum at the same time.

If it hadn't been for Dwight teaching me to change gears and to actually drive a car, I don't know when I would have gotten my driver's license. I was a pretty slow learner when it came to this driving stuff and I will always be grateful to him for his patience.

**My buddy Dwight and me**

I was almost seventeen years old before I got my driver's license. I was in no hurry. Daddy had an old, green, 1950 Plymouth that I called the "Green Bean". That was the car that I got to drive when I first started dating. Whoop-Ti-Doo! I never knew another living soul in the entire student body of Mooresville Senior High School that drove a Plymouth. Knowing that Richard Petty drove one, did somewhat assuage my embarrassment.

There was this particular, beige, 1953 Chevrolet that raced up and down Statesville Highway almost daily and I fell in love with that thing. I had been working at City Grocery and Market in downtown Mooresville for a while and thought that it was time for me to invest in my own set of wheels. (I wanted a car of my own—something terrible.) I was tired of driving that old Plymouth. I had already used some of my savings to reupholster the interior of the "Green Bean", but it still was not my own car. I wanted to experience the thrill of ownership like Roger had, but I wanted the outcome to be a little more profitable.

When I found out that the coveted Chevy was for sale, I sought out the owner, Ray Current. He had seen this car in a hot rod magazine and purchased it from a man from California. The Chevy had a 1957 Chevrolet grille and 1954 Chevy tail lights. It sported a beautiful pair of chrome lake-pipes down the sides and had been lowered to where it was just a few inches off the ground. Its exterior beauty was made complete by a set of Corvette hub-caps.

The interior had rolled-and-pleated leather upholstery and a custom made Toneau cover that fastened to the back of the front seat and extended all the way to the top of the back seat. The dashboard had all kind of special gauges and a dash-mounted tachometer. It was fitted with a 1958 Impala steering wheel to make it even sportier looking. Even the under side of the hood and the interior of the trunk was upholstered with the rolled-and-pleated leather. This was about the sportiest automobile to ever hit Mooresville.

The car boasted a 1958 truck motor with three carburetors and a racing cam. It had an electric fuel pump in the trunk that was activated by a switch on the dashboard. The gearshift was in the floor; and that just added to the car's allure.

I went to Piedmont Bank and talked to Mr. Bill Byrd about a loan for the car. I was only eighteen, but he finally gave in to my pleas, and loaned me four hundred and fifty dollars so I could buy the car of my dreams. I loved that car harder than a goat could butt a stump!

**My 1953 customized Chevrolet**

I was still driving it when I got married. My wife, Jean, never got the hang of changing the reversed gears in the floor. She was also a little vertically challenged and had to pull the seat up so far that she jammed the gear-knob into the front of the seat, so I decided to get a car that would be easier for her to drive. I drove that car for two or three years and sold the carburetors off of it for a hundred dollars and the electric fuel pump for another fifty dollars. I eventually sold the Chevy for four hundred and fifty dollars to Frank

Westmoreland. I think I came out pretty doggoned well for my first car.

**The interior of my dream car**

Frank drove that sharp little Chevy for a good while, and then sold it for $2500. The danged thing had become a classic!

# The Country Boy Today

You can take the boy out of the country, but you can't take the country out of the boy. I've heard that all my life, and I suppose that I am a living testimony to the truth of that old adage. I'm still about as country as I ever was—according to the people who hear me talk. I currently live within the city limits of Mooresville, but only about four miles from my childhood home. The other day, someone asked me if I have lived here all my life. I replied quickly, "Not yet."

My plan is to live out the rest of my days in my beloved community of Mooresville. I can't imagine living anywhere else. North Carolina is the right place for me—it always has been and always will be. I am a sentimental, dedicated, and loyal Tarheel. I guess the tar makes me stick close to my roots.

Growing up near Mooresville in the fifties was a true blessing. I learned from my parents that we didn't need everything under the sun to make us happy. We got by on a lot less than other folks, but I wonder if any of them were as happy as we were. We were as happy as if we had good sense. (I heard that a lot!)

I was always the runt of the family because of my asthma. I looked a lot younger than my actual age. Even after I started high school, I could still get into the movie theater for the price of a twelve year old.

I finally began putting on some weight when I reached the ninth grade. Mama took me to a specialist who prescribed allergy shots for my asthma. After taking shots for several months my condition improved considerably and I grew six inches in one year. Mama said that I ate everything in sight that didn't try to eat me. I told you earlier that I was always a hungry boy. Mama had to buy school clothes for me twice that year and we really couldn't afford it. I was amazed at how she made our money last like she did. God always provided for our needs, just like Daddy said He would.

I was very fortunate to have had caring teachers who nurtured me all through elementary school. I always liked to draw and was encouraged by many of my teachers to do so. Mrs. Nellie Brawley, my fourth grade teacher, asked me to draw and paint a scene across the top of the blackboard. I was thrilled to have the opportunity to use my talent—and on such a grand scale.

I painted a scene of Bethlehem and the surrounding desert. The camels didn't look so hot, but the palm trees and the buildings turned out rather nicely, and everyone seemed pleased.

Our teachers would invariably ask everyone in the class what we wanted to be when we grew up, and I was always quick to reply that I wanted to be an artist. They very kindly told me that it would be better if I learned a trade because it would be difficult to make a living as an artist. I assumed they were correct; after all, they were my teachers.

I liked to draw cars, airplanes, buildings, and landscapes, but architectural subjects were my specialty. Creating a natural looking tree was always a challenge for me. Joyce Kilmer said it best in his poem, when he wrote, "Only God can make a tree." I know I really had a lot of trouble creating one when I was in school. Painting trees today has become fun and I think that I finally have gotten the hang of it.

I continued my love for drawing into high school and remember drawing and designing automobiles while in study hall. At one time I thought that I wanted to be an automotive designer.

During my drafting and mechanical drawing classes in high school, I found that I really liked the challenge of drawing house plans. Mr. Conard Tharpe was my teacher and encouraged me, even though at times I gave him a lot of grief with my classroom antics. I took those skills I learned in his class and later designed and drew the plans for two of my own homes. I realized that architecture can be beautiful, and that instilled within me a desire to create.

Still lacking direction in my senior year, I knew I would soon have to find some kind of job. One day I was looking out the window during my Geography class watching my buddy, Dwight Neill digging a trench in the hard ground to bury some electrical lines. He had graduated the year before and already had a real job working for George B. Stevens Electrical Company as an electrician's helper. They were building the Roland R. Morgan Auditorium, and my class was to be the first to graduate in it. I thought to my self, maybe I could do that.

Well, when I graduated in 1962, Dwight helped me get a job as an electrician's helper, doing the same thing he did. I was assigned to work with Sloan Westmoreland, so I could learn all about being an electrician. He asked me, "Do you know anything about earth moving equipment?" I replied that I did not, but I was willing to learn. I was immediately handed a shovel! I knew right then that I was not in my chosen profession. I stuck in there for a few months but soon realized that this manual labor stuff and I didn't bond very well.

I eventually went to work at Draymore Manufacturing Company. Dwight is still in the electrical business today. He has the responsible position of project manager for Overcash Electric Company in Mooresville.

While working at Draymore, I met Jean Coone, from Davidson, and we married in October of 1963. After working there a few years, I went back to the job that I had during high school—working at City Grocery and Market.

I really learned a lot working in the grocery business and enjoyed every minute of it. We had fun every day. Working at the store also helped me to develop confidence. I was soon put in charge of purchasing the produce. I worked alongside John McLean in the meat market too and learned to cut up a chicken in less than thirty seconds. John taught me things about working with the public that I have never forgotten. John McLean was not only my boss, but a great friend. The things I learned about customer service while working at City Grocery has served me well throughout my career as a small business owner.

In February of 1968, I left City Grocery and Market and went to work in the boy's department at Belk's Department Store. I was later moved to the men's department where Ross Brown was my boss. He worked for Belk's for forty or fifty years and was a great inspiration to me. Ross taught me a lot about merchandising, selling, and inventory control. Bob Edmiston worked with us in the men's department too, and together we were a great team.

Jean and I had two wonderful daughters together. Susan was born in September of 1967 and Karen came along on Christmas Eve in 1976.

Daddy had a massive heart attack and passed away on July 6, 1970. He was only 57 years old. Everyone was shocked and saddened by his sudden death and kept talking about how young he was. Young—I thought he was an old man! I was only twenty-five years old at the time of his death. I have already lived five years longer than he did and I definitely don't think I'm old!

Mother was seven years younger than Daddy. She lived to see me realize my dream of becoming an artist. Mama even worked at my gallery in the early 1990's when I was traveling. She passed away on April 30, 1995 after a long battle with cancer.

The days my parents passed away were the two of the saddest ones of my life, and I miss them every single day. It doesn't matter how old you are when you lose your parents—you immediately become an orphan and loose your link to the past. They are no longer there to answer questions about how you are related to "so and so". They are not available for sound advice, and they are no longer there to visit or to hold and nurture your children. They are only available in our memories. Thank God for them!

While working at Belk's, I took a drawing course through Mitchell Community College. The course lasted ten or twelve nights. After going for two or three lessons, I was becoming frustrated because we continued drawing the same way each night. I remember asking the instructor, Don Chapman, to help me learn how to add a new dimension to my drawing. Don showed me how to shade my subjects from light to dark. It was as if a light turned on in my brain—I then understood how to accomplish what I had been trying to do. I thanked him and started drawing with a newly inspired purpose. He had me helping other students by the sixth night. Don actually believed that I could become an artist and told me so! I had needed to hear those words for almost thirty years. I will always be grateful to him for his encouragement and confidence in me.

Bob Edmiston and I spent our days off together and hunted for old bottles for my collection. One day, we were treasure hunting at his grandfather's deserted house. Bob promised me all the bottles we found that day if I would draw a picture of the old Edmiston home-place. That sounded good to me, so I sat on the trunk of my old Buick LeSabre and sketched my first commissioned work. Bob's mother, Frances, had the drawing framed. Her neighbor, Mrs. Davidson, saw it, and asked me if I would draw her house. She was willing to pay; and that, dear friends, was the humble beginning of my art career.

Ray Boone managed the shoe department at Belk's and challenged me to become a better salesperson, a better musician, a better artist, and a better citizen. He was always encouraging me to excel in any endeavor in which I was involved. He had me reading books that were thought provoking and studying history. We trout fished, hunted arrowheads, took an archeology course, camped out and hiked together.

Ray always had ideas that I would never had thought of on my own. Mama had been writing a pen pal in England for over twenty-seven years but never had gotten to meet her in person. Ray challenged me to paint a watercolor and sell it for $500 to buy Mama a round-trip ticket to England. I did as he instructed and was able to buy Mama the plane ticket. Roger and Laura pitched in some spending money for her and she had a once-in-a-lifetime experience of spending three weeks in England with her friends. She talked about that trip until her death. I would never have come up with such a fabulous idea without Ray's suggestion.

**Ray Boone trout fishing the easy way**

Vickie and I went to Maine in 2000 and arranged to meet Ray, and his wife Betty, in Boothbay Harbor. We spent five or six days driving them along the coast of Maine; showing them the lighthouses and lobster villages that have inspired me for years. I am grateful to have had that opportunity. Ray passed away last year and I was one of the pallbearers at his funeral. I cried as we sang *I'll Fly Away* at his graveside. I hope I am doing him proud by writing this book.

Many kind people helped me on my journey to becoming an artist. Nancy Frazier gave me a sheet of watercolor paper and loaned me her watercolors and brushes. She then challenged me to paint. I had never seen anyone paint a watercolor before, but nonetheless, I gave it a shot. Blackwelder's Store in Amity Hill, North Carolina was the subject of my first painting. Everybody wanted to buy it! I couldn't believe it! It took me a year to save enough money to buy the needed supplies, to paint another picture. You have to remember that I was working at Belk's.

**My first watercolor of Blackwelder's store**

I began painting seriously while still working there and had some of my originals on display in my office located in the men's department. I found painting to be fun and exciting, but the most rewarding thing was to know that what I was doing was being appreciated.

Fletcher Davis, a local photographer of note, saw my paintings and suggested that I go to the Outer Banks of North Carolina. He insisted that I see for myself, the beauty of the windswept dunes, the pounding surf, and the imposing, lighthouses. I will always be indebted to him for his wise counsel.

I visited the Banks for the first time in 1980 and found myself standing in the shadow of the majestic Cape Hatteras Lighthouse. That was the moment I decided to pursue my career in fine art.

I also felt an obligation to use my God-given talent to capture as many of our landmarks on paper as I can, before they disappear forever.

I returned home and resigned my position as menswear buyer at Belk's. (I would have quit earlier, but unemployment compensation would have put me in a higher income bracket.)

**My painting of Cape Hatteras Lighthouse**

For six years, I struggled to make a living in a one-room gallery, located upstairs over Kelly Clothing Company in downtown Mooresville. My little gallery was directly across the street from Belk's, and I looked out of my window quite often at my previous place of employment and wondered if I had done the right thing. Many loyal customers from Belk's would come to my gallery and ask me to go to the men's department with them to help pick out their neckties. I was not the only one having trouble adjusting to my severance with Belk's Department Store. I really think everyone there thought that I would eventually return and ask for my old job back.

Jean and I went our separate ways after twenty-three years of marriage. It was a difficult time for all of us in the mid 1980's. Jean was, and still is, a fine woman and deserved much better than me. We remain friends and see each other at our grandchildren's birthday parties and other occasions. Jean has remarried and lives in Rowan County near Woodleaf. She enjoys being a grandmother and dotes on her grandchildren.

I never gave up and never quit painting, and gradually my business grew. I moved my gallery downstairs to 212 North Main Street in February of 1987. I married Vickie Edwards in March of that year; and she went to work with me and began managing the gallery. Vickie has been my encouragement, inspiration, and helpmate for the last nineteen years. She works harder than anyone else I know, helping me continue my dream. I would not be where I am today without her advice, ideas, and her unwavering faith in my ability. She always challenges me to do nothing less than my best. She must have learned that from Ray Boone.

Vickie has three children that we have raised together, and it has been quite an eventful life. Her daughter, Lisa, and sons, Greg and Darrin, are all grown now and are making their marks in the world.

Lisa graduated from The University of North Carolina at Greensboro and began teaching fourth grade at South Elementary School in Mooresville. There, she met Chuck

LaRusso, who was also a teacher. They married in 1999 and now Lisa is a stay-at-home mom with an extremely active three-year old daughter, Caroline, and a brand new set of identical twin girls, Chloe and Claire. Chuck is now the director of the exceptional children's program for the Mooresville Graded School District. Lisa has the privilege of staying home to be with her growing family. Sometimes I think she would like to work just to get some rest.

Vickie's oldest son, Greg graduated from Campbell University and married Mary Beth Cash. They have a son, Aidan, who is an active two-year old boy. Greg is currently working in the construction business while Mary Beth works at *Chili's Bar and Grill.* Greg and Mary Beth live near Denver, North Carolina.

Darrin, the youngest, graduated from East Carolina University in May, 2006 and is pursuing a career in the shipping industry. Darrin is training at different ports on the Atlantic seaboard and will be involved in international shipping. We are proud of all of them and their successes.

**Mary Beth, Aidan, Darrin in back, Greg, Vickie and Gigi, Lisa, Caroline, and Chuck Larusso**

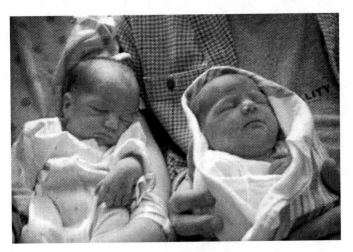

**The Twins: Chloe and Claire**

Gigi, our five year old SRM (Spoiled Rotten Maltese), came to live with us in 2002 when Vickie's mom passed away. Gigi was already spoiled by the time we assumed responsibility for her and has just gotten worse. She is not only a part of our family, but has become a great favorite of our customers at the gallery. Sometimes, they come to the gallery just to see Gigi. She has added lots of joy to our home and business. I call her the Wonder Dog, because we really wonder what she is going to do next.

**Gigi, the Wonder Dog**

My oldest daughter, Susan has two children from a previous marriage. Dustin graduated from South Iredell High School in June, 2006. He will be attending North Carolina State University. Kristian is a rising junior at South Iredell High School high school and is a knockout. They both are extremely intelligent young people.

Susan and her husband Michael Koury added to their family with the birth of Cassie and Will. Cassie is a beautiful six year old girl that takes dance and is smart as a whip. Will is a delightful two-year old that makes us laugh by keeping his tongue stuck out.

Susan is the practice manager for Sanger Clinic and Mike is an engineer for the town of Mooresville.

**Susan and husband Mike Koury, Kristian, Will, Dustin, and Cassie**

My youngest daughter, Karen is the proud mother of Lucas Barbee, an active five-year old boy that loves to play outside. He is all "boy" and is a lot like his papaw when it comes to that eating habit. Karen is currently a single-mom and is living in Mooresville. She is employed in the printing industry and works in Mooresville.

**Karen and Lucas Barbee**

Vickie and I are very fortunate in having all of our children living nearby. We now have a total of nine grandchildren. Is it any wonder that I am tired? We stay busy just acknowledging the birthdays, Christmas and other special occasions.

So far, Vickie and I have traveled to forty-four of our United States and several provinces of Canada. It is my goal to paint a watercolor from each of the places we have visited.

We plan to go to California and visit Yosemite National Park and drive up the Pacific Coastal Highway. I want to visit the Haceta Head Lighthouse on the coast of Oregon and the dramatic Olympic Peninsula of Washington State. Hopefully, the trip will include sightseeing in British Columbia and Banff National Park in Canada before driving through North Dakota on the way home. Then, that will about do it for me. I will have driven to all the forty-eight contiguous states and seven provinces of Canada.

I never tire of driving to Maine and enjoying the beauty of its rocky coast. I also love the West and go there as often as possible. Traveling is such a necessary part of being an artist. The natural beauty of our country inspires and refreshes my soul.

**On the rocks: Pemaquid, Maine**

We drive everywhere we go, and that takes a lot of time, but I have read in the Bible where it plainly states: "Lo, I will be with you always." It doesn't say anything about being with me while I am thirty thousand feet in the air on a US AIR jet.

I do enjoy flying in small planes, but now that I am older, I don't think I have the patience for the hassle experienced at the large airports. I should have started flying commercially when I was younger. It would probably help if I weren't so stubborn, but I really enjoy driving. I like to see the changes in the topography as we drive from state to state. America is a big, beautiful country, and I want to see it all. My dream is to drive to Alaska.

One of the biggest thrills I ever had was visiting Monument Valley, Arizona and spending the night at Goulding's Trading Post. We drove down into the valley in the late evening and were awed by the natural beauty of the setting. I could almost see John Wayne leading the cavalry charge across the desert with the majestic, red-rock monuments as a backdrop.

**At Monument Valley, Arizona**

My goal is to paint a picture from all one hundred counties in North Carolina and one from each of the forty-eight contiguous states. I am well on my way and am enjoying myself as I go.

The last twenty-five years have gone by so quickly. I have traveled and painted scenes from all over the United States. Last year, I tried my hand at oil painting. My first oil, entitled, *Last Curve to Buffalo,* was an autumn scene of a country road in Ashe County, North Carolina. My second oil painting was of the magnificent Monument Valley of Arizona.

I have always enjoyed writing poetry and songs, and I began playing the guitar in the 1960's. My good friend, Johnny Freeze taught me the chords, and we used to play together every chance we got. Jean bought a flattop, acoustic Gibson guitar for me back in the early '60's, and I still play it today. My ability is somewhat lacking, but the enjoyment is still there. I occasionally play Bluegrass music with a talented bunch of folks on Monday nights. I am always asked to sing with them, but I am quick to respond, "The only singer we had in our house was a sewing machine."

I wrote a poem entitled, *O' My Jesus* in 1975 about Good Friday and Jesus' death on the cross. A good friend of mine, Tim Brown, set it to music. The lyrics accompanied by the haunting melody; reminds us of Jesus' sacrifice on the cross. *O' My Jesus* has been sung in many local churches and is one of my accomplishments of which I am most proud.

God has been good to me and blessed me with a talent of which I did nothing to deserve. He blessed me with a good family and the love and support of my community. What more could a man desire?

I was honored in 2001 to receive the prestigious *Order of the Long Leaf Pine* from Governor Mike Easley. This award is the highest civilian honor that can be granted in the state of North Carolina. I will always treasure the award and was humbled to have been one of its recipients. In 2004, I was chosen as the featured artist for the North Carolina Governor's Conference on Tourism. I feel very fortunate to have been born and raised in North Carolina and I am grateful for its natural beauty that has inspired many of my paintings.

I retired in July 2006 and turned over the responsibilities of running the business to Vickie who is far more capable than I ever was. We have a very professional staff at our gallery to assist Vickie and that will allow me time off to explore forgotten country roads.

I am currently working on my first novel and that has been both interesting and challenging. I have written a guide that leads visitors through New England and along the dramatic, rocky coast of Maine with its numerous lighthouses, and quaint lobster villages. The book carefully directs the reader to Campobello, Island in Canada, and then through some of the most peaceful villages of New Hampshire and Vermont and back home again.

A travel guide for the Outer Banks of North Carolina has also been completed and is available at the gallery.

Photography has always been a hobby of mine and now that I have a new digital, single-lens reflex camera, I hope to be on the back roads of America more often, clicking away. I want to travel more, paint when I feel like it, and play a little music on Saturdays at the Cook Shack in Union Grove. I want to take my grandchildren on long country drives and share the beauty of North Carolina with them before it changes beyond recognition. I want to read at least two books a week and volunteer more of my time to civic work.

I plan on staying active in the Mooresville/Lake Norman Exchange Club and working diligently with its club members and volunteers on the "Cotton" Ketchie Arts Festival. This annual event in downtown Mooresville showcases the works of artisans across North Carolina and raises money for the prevention of child abuse. In addition to the prevention of child abuse, the Exchange Club also focuses on community service, Americanism, and youth programs. I joined this very worthwhile organization in the late 1990's as another way to give back to my community, but truly believe I have received far more than I have ever given.

I was chosen as Exchangite of the Year for the North Carolina District in 2004. I was extremely honored to have received this recognition from among the thirty-five clubs totaling over nine hundred members.

**2004 Exchangite of the Year for North Carolina**

Vickie and I serve on the Board of Directors for Iredell County's Exchange/SCAN Child and Parenting Center. The center was incorporated in 1991 for the purpose of preventing parents from abusing and neglecting their children, and intervening when abuse has occurred. Here, moms and dads learn to be better parents by nurturing their children instead of abusing them. The SCAN Center is the recipient of the proceeds from the Cotton Ketchie Arts Festival.

I also intend to remain a member of the Mooresville/Lake Norman Rotary Club and actively support the works they do, not only in our community, but around the world. As a Paul Harris Fellow, I am especially proud of this group of dedicated business men and women.

Vickie and I were honored to furnish framed prints for the offices of North Carolina Senator Elizabeth Dole in both Raleigh and Salisbury. Meeting her was a very special moment in the life of this old country boy.

**Senator Elizabeth Dole, Vickie, and me**

From the picture below, you can see why they call me "Cotton". My hair was white most of my life but darkened somewhat as I grew older. Now, doggone it, the stuff has gotten white again, (its thinner in spots, too.)

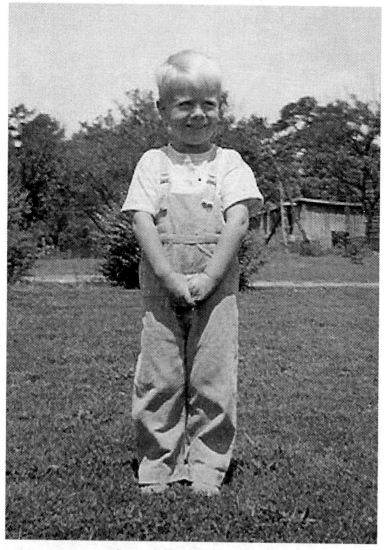

**Now, you know why they call me "Cotton"**

**Today at the Gallery**

It was only by the grace of God that I was fortunate enough to have been born in North Carolina and raised in the country. I am also thankful to have been born in the 1940's. I have witnessed the infancy of television, the birth of personal computers, and the excitement of men walking on the moon. I have enjoyed dating at the drive-in-theater, eating fifteen cent hot dogs, building ponds in the pasture, hunting for possums, rabbits, and squirrels, having fun at Brown's Skating Rink and Swimming Pool, playing games with my family instead of Nintendo, and fishing in the old Catawba River. The list could go on and on, but I think by now, you may have an idea that I'm happy that I was raised where I was and am happy being who I am.

I will probably remain my same, old self and do the same old things until they carry me away. I don't do change very well—so I've been told. I don't see any reason to start now!